M000032087

INTRODUCTION
TO
ESTATE PLANNING

How to Protect and
Pass on Your Legacy

Published by Bardolf & Company

INTRODUCTION TO ESTATE PLANNING
How to Protect and Pass on Your Legacy

ISBN 978-1-938842-35-1

Copyright © 2017 Keith Tokerud

All rights reserved. No part of this book may be used or repro-
duced in any form or by any electronic or mechanical means,
including information storage and retrieval systems, without
permission in writing from the publisher.

For information write:

Bardolf & Company
5430 Colewood Pl.
Sarasota, FL 34232
941-232-0113

Printed in the United States of America

Cover design by Shawcreative

Note: This book is intended for educational and informational
purposes only. It is not intended to act as legal advice.

To
Becky and Hannah

INTRODUCTION
TO
ESTATE PLANNING

How to Protect and
Pass on Your Legacy

Keith Tokerud

Bardolf & Company
Sarasota, Florida

Table of Contents

Introduction

Planning: It Can Make a Difference

My great grandfather was born in Norway and worked as a stone mason there before moving to Montana and homesteading. He wasn't that great with English, but he was a hard worker, and he made a success of his grain and cattle ranch.

My dad and he were very close. My dad was five when his parents divorced, and he spent most of his childhood on his grandparents' farm. He wasn't jealous when his aunts and uncle got to stay in town to attend school or when they went away to college. He loved the farm.

After a stint in the Army my dad moved to town, but my great grandfather would often call for help, and my dad would spend the weekend fixing the tractor or hauling cattle to market.

When my great grandfather couldn't handle the place anymore, he turned to my dad. The understanding was that my dad could start out leasing and eventually take over the farm.

So my dad brought my mom out to the farm. There was no written lease. (That wasn't necessary, since it was family!) My dad renovated the farmhouse and outbuildings, repaired the fence, upgraded the equipment and bought cattle. Everything went great.

Then my great grandfather died.

He left everything to his wife. No mention of the farm or my dad. My dad wasn't as close to his grandmother as he'd been to his grandfather, but they got along fine. Still, when one of my dad's newly married aunts came home and asked to take over the farm, that was it: the end of my dad's farming. At the end of the year he had to move back to town.

Forty years later my dad was still upset. He didn't show his emotions openly, but it was obvious how much he felt the loss. I've often wondered how his life—and mine—would have been different if my great grandfather had done good estate planning.

What I See Every Day

Every day I see the results of inadequate estate planning. Successful, business-like people have passed away without doing any planning, or they've left outdated documents that don't address the important issues facing their heirs. They've left a mess for their families to clean up. That means more headache and expense for their families. And, all too often, it means disputes between family members that are never resolved.

Happily, I also get to sit down with clients who are willing to do the kind of planning necessary to avoid such sad results. As these clients leave the office after signing their estate planning documents, many exclaim how good they feel. They say they have peace of mind, and I can tell that they're proud that they've taken care of themselves and their family. It makes me feel proud and happy that I've been able to help.

What is Estate Planning?

So, what is "estate planning," anyway? I've heard it described as a deliberate, premeditated act of love. I can't communicate in such terms myself (being of Norwegian heritage), but I do believe that you plan your estate because you really care about your family. It can be one of the most important things you do for yourself and your family.

I define estate planning by saying:

"I want to control my property while I'm alive and well, take care of myself and my family if I become disabled, and give what I have to whom I want, the way I want, and when I want. Furthermore, I want to save every last tax dollar, professional fee and court cost legally possible."

There is a lot packed into that definition. First, whatever we do, you should end up feeling that you have more control than you did before the planning.

Good estate planning doesn't just benefit your family. Good estate planning helps you maintain control. That means more power to make the decisions that affect your health and your property. More authority and more options. Ultimately, it means more dignity.

So, while you're healthy and going about your business, your planning should be invisible. It shouldn't complicate your life or limit your ability to do whatever you want. Then, when you need it, the planning should kick in without delay, controversy or expense to make sure that your wishes are followed even if something has happened to you.

Of course, estate planning deals with death. However, statistically you are more likely to become disabled than to die in any given year. So, your estate planning should help you maintain control if you become disabled. For, instance, how do we decide if your condition is serious enough that you are "incapacitated"? Who will make that call? A judge who has never met you? And, if that call is made, who will handle your affairs? You should be the one making these decisions ahead of time, not someone else when it's too late for you to have any input.

Then, yes, when you are gone, good estate planning means that what you wanted to happen does happen—with no family disputes and with no unnecessary expenses or complications. It should protect your family from "creditors and predators" (people who want to take your family's money, such as plaintiffs in lawsuits and ex-spouses).

Approach your Planning in Stages

When you first sit down to talk about your estate planning you're liable to feel overwhelmed. There's so much to consider! So, start with your basic planning and get that in place first. Then you can address issues such as lifetime gifting, transferring the family farm or setting up irrevocable trusts. Here's what I suggest:

1. Start with putting together your estate planning team.

2. Then take the time to carefully define your goals. Of course, these will relate to disposition of your property, but don't forget about your healthcare.

3. Decide who should be authorized to know about your medical condition if something happens to you. Who do you want to make medical decisions for you if you can't? And, if you are at death's doorstep, what kind of medical care do you want?

4. Then, consider incapacity issues involving your financial affairs. What do you want to happen if you become incapacitated? Who should be involved, and what should they do? Where do you want to spend your last years?

5. And, finally, decide who should handle your affairs and what they should do when you pass away. Who should receive your property and under what conditions?

This is your basic planning. Once you have answered these questions, we can decide what legal tools to use to implement your wishes. Depending on your circumstances, that may be all the planning you need to do. If there are other issues you want to deal with, we will tackle them once your basic planning is in place.

For instance, if you have a large, complex estate, it may make sense to start transitioning management and ownership now rather than when you pass away. It might also make sense to establish legal entities such as trusts and to start transferring assets to them now. This will allow you to maintain control while you educate and gradually transfer authority to the next generation. It may also save taxes.

CHAPTER 1

Choosing Your Estate Planning Team

The Importance of a Team

You will do your best planning if you work with a team. You want the expertise that different professionals bring to the table. A team also helps in a very practical way: getting something done! It doesn't do much good to design a great estate plan if you never put it in place. Planning with a team will help you stay the course to implement your plan and actually do something for you and your family.

The Members of Your Team

You will need an attorney. The attorney will be primarily responsible for the documents, diagrams, asset ownership arrangements and beneficiary designations. The attorney is usually also the "quarterback" of your planning team. He or she will be responsible for the logistics (setting up meetings, distributing meeting minutes and other documents, communicating constantly with you to make sure you're happy with the process).

Although your attorney may be most familiar with the "nuts and bolts" of the planning strategies, your other advisors will likely have important ideas to contribute. Of course, a lot of planning relates to taxes. Now, with the high federal estate tax exemption, income tax planning is more important than ever, and that's the accountant's forte.

You may have been working with your accountant for many years. If so, your accountant not only knows a lot about your business and financial affairs but also your family and personal issues. The accountant can help by raising important issues that you either haven't focused on or just have forgotten to mention.

Your financial advisor also may know a lot about your family and issues that should be dealt with in planning. Further, your estate planning needs to take into account not only the size of your estate but its composition. Many times life insurance is something to at least consider. Your financial advisor or life insurance agent is the expert on that.

It's great if all your advisors actually attend meetings with you and your attorney. At a minimum you should authorize and encourage your attorney to keep your advisors in the loop and to solicit their advice throughout the process.

We'll discuss later how important it is to keep your plan up to date. Your team members can also help with that. In my office we have an updating process, The Peace of Mind Protector, that I'll explain later. An important part of the process is keeping your other advisors informed so we can all help you adjust and improve your planning over time.

You Need Team Players

Your team is only going to work if the team members respect one another and rely upon one another. This is not always easy for professionals! We lawyers are especially famous for outsized egos.

By the same token accountants are by reputation conservative and not outgoing. They're often not used to working in teams with other professionals. Financial advisors may be reluctant to work with lawyers and accountants, whom financial advisors and insurance salesman often see as "deal killers."

The professionals need to get over this and to work as a team for you.

A Jack of all Trades?

The most important estate planning team member will be your attorney. How do you choose him or her?

Every lawyer, it seems, says that he or she does "estate planning." This often means that they prepare simple wills and powers of attorney taken from a form book. You don't want that kind of planning if you are really concerned about your family and your legacy.

You want to deal with someone who focuses on estate planning and related topics like long-term care planning and business succession planning day in and day out and who has the in-depth knowledge to help you navigate this complicated terrain.

My "New Me" Story

What else is important about your lawyer? To answer that, let me tell you how I used to approach estate planning.

I practiced with my father-in-law, whose philosophy was to work with whoever came in the door, whether we were a good fit or not.

If clients said they wanted their planning to be "simple," I thought that meant that my job was to sit right down, ask the client what he or she wanted and to draft short documents that stuck to the points the client had mentioned. Short meetings and short documents.

Then along came my midlife crisis. I started asking myself questions like: "How am I spending my life?" "Am I making a difference?" "Am I really helping people?" I didn't like the answers I was giving myself.

I decided that I wasn't helping clients with their most important issues. I was basically just being a scribe. Yes, my clients ended up with planning that covered the points they had raised, but they didn't end up with planning that gave them the best chance of keeping control of their lives and passing on their legacy.

So, now I focus on what I came to realize is the most important part of the planning process: working through the essential questions about what is important besides financial wealth—and how we can enhance each family member's life. This meant that I need to be interested in and take the time to really understand my clients' goals, families, problems, to help them identify what is most important to them. It may sound a little grandiose, but by doing this I began to help my clients discover and develop their capacity to achieve greater effectiveness and significance.

I try to ask the right questions, to provide knowledge—breadth as well as depth—to demonstrate big picture thinking as well as analysis and to listen rather than just tell. I want to provide new perspectives and new ways of looking at the same old issues. To help my clients see the big picture.

My Family's Dentists

I used to work like my dad's dentist worked. Today I work like my own dentist works.

My dad went to the dentist whenever he thought he needed to. If a tooth was bothering him he went. He told the dentist what he wanted. "I need a filling on this tooth." Or "I need this tooth pulled."

The dentist filled the tooth or pulled it right then and charged what my dad thought was a fair price. My dad thought he was getting good care. There was one little problem, though: my dad ended up with false teeth.

I don't just go to my dentist when I think I have a problem. And he doesn't just do whatever I tell him and then send me home. He has a process to maintain my dental health that starts with regular check-ups. So, he finds problems that I'm not even aware of and treats them before they get serious. If I do go in with a specific complaint, he listens patiently to what I say. But he doesn't just accept what I say and start pulling teeth. He does an examination and tells me what he thinks I need. He's not just an "order taker." His recommendation may be very different from what I thought I needed, but I generally follow his advice. I'm getting great care. Of course, I'm paying more than my dad did, and I'm seeing my dentist more often than my dad saw his. But I'll bet you I never end up with false teeth.

You Want an Attorney who Listens

You want an attorney who will really listen to you. Shouldn't be that hard to find one, right? Not so!

All too often attorneys assume that it's their job to do their clients' thinking for them and just to tell the clients what to do. They see themselves as the experts on what their clients should do and think. But real help is giving people the framework in which to generate their own ideas first.

You may not know what you want or need for your estate planning. You haven't had the opportunity to really think about your planning or to verbalize your thoughts. You may not really know how you feel about things. And, yes, there are a number of issues involved in estate planning that you probably don't know about.

But, usually the brain that contains the problem also contains the solution—often the best one. That means that, with help from your attorney, you will be the one who comes up with the best answers.

So, you want an attorney who wants to know what you think, who you are, and what matters to you. It is critical that your attorney be able—and willing—to really listen to you. Without interruptions. Without offering advice before all the facts and concerns are on the table. And without talking just to show how smart or knowledgeable he or she is. That means the most important expertise in the attorney you want to work with is the ability to generate your finest independent thinking.

You Should be in Control

Once your attorney has really listened and helped you uncover your most important concerns, then it's the attorney's job to bring solutions to the table. All your planning team members will have suggestions about what you should do and how you should do it. They will be familiar with jargon that is new—and confusing—to you. Hopefully they'll be good at explaining their ideas.

But it must be clear throughout who is in charge of your planning: you. No matter what, everyone should agree upfront and be constantly working to maintain your control of the process throughout.

That means that you understand the process, that your advisors give you the benefit of their thoughts in language you can understand, that you and your advisors take as long as necessary to flesh out the issues and gain clarity on what to do about them, and that you understand your planning documents and other "deliverables." In other words that the end product is your plan, not anyone else's.

Any time you feel out of control or confused, the process is not working properly. Fixing the problem may be as simple as taking a few minutes to go over a tax concept using a diagram. Or it may be as serious as your advisors trying to foist upon you a plan that you're not comfortable with but feel helpless to resist.

Understandable English and Diagrams

Part of staying in control is understanding what people are saying and writing. Lawyers deal in written documents using specialized legal jargon that is hard to understand, right? That may be true generally, but it shouldn't be for your estate planning lawyer.

It's not up to you to guess what arcane words and concepts mean. It's up to your attorney to explain so that you understand. Your attorney needs to speak and write in understandable English to make sure you and everyone else involved knows how your planning is to work. The idea is not to make the attorney look smart. It's to communicate clearly so that you feel like you've been heard and that you truly understand the solutions being suggested.

So, documents that use language that you understand is the minimum. In my office we take it to the next step and use diagrams to describe how your plan will work. It's amazing how much clearer your planning is when you can see a picture of how it works. We've found our diagrams to be helpful to our clients and also a great tool to use when we meet later with family members who haven't been involved in the planning process.

You Want an Attorney who Follows a Process

I have one more suggestion about how you can stay in control. Work with an attorney who follows a defined process. Estate planning is too complicated for you and your team to just bounce around from topic to topic in never-ending conversations. Using a defined process will help you identify the most important issues and get your planning done in a timely and efficient manner. It may have taken you a while to finally sit down to do estate planning. Part of your attorney's job is to help you get your planning done without any more delay.

Working through a process will allow you to always know what's going on and where you're headed. That will allow you to feel in control. You will know what the planning will involve, what the steps are, what each party's responsibilities are, how long the process will last and, of course, what it will cost. That way at each step you'll be able to make the best decisions. I've outlined my own process in Chapter 16 below.

You can also learn more about our process on our website, *www.MontanaEstateLawyer.com.*

CHAPTER 2

Defining Your Goals

Your Job is to Share your Concerns

Good planning starts with identifying goals. Your goals! Not other people's goals or what someone thinks your goals should be.

Rather than rushing into a discussion about saving taxes or what to do about the family cabin, we want to take the time to figure out what you want to achieve. I find that many clients have never had the opportunity to really think about their goals.

So, your job is to share what your goals and concerns really are. The discussion should take as long as necessary. No rushing, no deadlines, no impatience. If we are going to do valuable planning we need to take the time to think about and discuss the issues that are keeping you awake at night as well as to identify the issues you may not have thought about. We don't want to jump to solutions till we know what the problems are.

Sounds pretty simple, doesn't it? Well, it isn't. But if we can work like this, we can do some great planning!

It's all about Control and Legacy

When we ask our clients about their estate planning goals, many first mention saving taxes. But as we go through our process with clients to help them identify and really understand their most important issues, we almost always end up wrestling with issues of control and legacy. (Taxes resurface as part of the legacy conversation. Our clients usually want to give more to their family and less to the government. We'll come to that in Chapter 17.)

Good estate planning is based on keeping you in control of your life whenever possible. As we age, we lose control. Our bodies begin to fail us. We start to experience more and more "senior moments." And change is everywhere. Technological changes make what was once simple impossible (see: TV remotes, opening bottles). Our finances drift uncontrollably with economic downturns and impossibly low rates of return.

Maintaining control can mean many things, starting with funding your retirement and providing for family emergencies. You have worked hard many years and built up an estate. You want to enjoy it yourself—you're still here, by the way!

The "golden years" are also a time when we look back. We naturally dwell more and more on the meaning of our lives. What difference have we made? What have we accomplished? When we're gone, what will we leave behind? What is our legacy?

Our planning discussion may lead you to a fundamental question that you've never thought of: "What is the purpose for our family's wealth?"

Most of us want to help provide a higher standard of living for family members. That may mean freeing up some family members to choose careers based on factors other than economics. Often it means doing what we can to make a family business survive and thrive. And you may decide that you have enough to also provide resources for philanthropy.

All of this relates to your financial legacy. But isn't part of your legacy non-financial? I would argue that it's the most important part. You've tried hard to raise your family with values that will hold them in good stead. As they age, you rightfully expect them to pass these values on to the next generation. That means passing on family history, passing on life's lessons, leaving behind something of what your life has meant. So, a goal of your estate planning can be to flesh this out, to identify and enhance the legacy you want to leave behind.

Common Estate Planning Goals

As you think about your family members, at bottom you probably just want them to be happy and to have a better life as a result of your planning than they would have otherwise. Our job will thus be to figure out what happiness and a better life look like from both your perspective and theirs.

Of course, you want to specify who is to receive your estate and under what circumstances. You may own special assets such as a cabin or a family business (in Montana where I live, often a farm or ranch) that you want to pass on to some family members while also providing a fair share of your estate to others. If, like my great grandfather, you want your grandson to take over the family farm, your planning should address that, rather than leaving the issue up in the air.

Once you decide who should get what, the question is how you should pass it on. Do you want to begin transferring assets during your lifetime? Should you transfer them outright or in some type of protective arrangement such as a trust? Should you designate someone to help heirs who are too young or are simply incapable of managing their inheritance? Again, what will make your heirs' lives better in the long run as a result of your planning?

You may also be concerned about runaway medical and nursing home expenses eating up your savings. If so, you want to do what I call "Long-Term Care Planning." It's a whole topic unto itself that traditional estate planning doesn't directly address. We will cover that in Chapter 5.

And what about where you'll live as you get older? There's a new field called "Aging in Place" devoted to helping you stay at home as you age if that's what you want. See Chapter 6.

Avoiding a Family Dispute

Can you imagine a grandson hitting his grandfather with his pickup and then leaving him out in the country in winter with a broken hip? I can imagine it very clearly because it happened to one of our elderly clients.

Our client had been very successful in business and was able to bring his two kids, let's call them Bob and Allen, into the business as partners, transferring millions of dollars of business assets to them, while he was still alive. The problem was that both kids worked in the business, but Bob was more active, and he resented Allen's receiving the same compensation as he. When Bob complained to his father about this, his father invariably took Allen's side, incensing Bob. Bob's boys joined the company and took their dad's side, eventually becoming estranged from their grandfather and their uncle. Things got worse and worse until, on a cold December afternoon, Bob's son left his injured grandfather out in the country, cussing at him as he drove away.

That is an extreme example of what can happen when a parent doesn't handle a business transition well. Never happen in your family, I'm sure, but shouldn't one of your goals be to minimize family disputes when you're gone? Many of our clients have seen these fights tear up a family and want to make sure it doesn't happen to their family. All too often, though, when I bring up the topic, my clients assure me that their family is different, there will never be fights, so we don't need to worry about that as we do their planning.

That can be a big mistake. When a parent has died or become incapacitated, jealousy and hurt feelings from the distant past often flare up and drive a wedge between siblings who seemed to get along fine while their parents were still doing well. I really believe every parent should address this issue in their planning. What do you think?

CHAPTER 3

Healthcare Planning

No matter what your age or health status, you ought to have healthcare planning documents in place. That way, if you can't make your own decisions about your healthcare, someone whom you trust can make the decisions for you. The tools we use for this are:

- a healthcare power of attorney,
- a living will, and
- an authorization for release of medical information (HIPAA Release).

The Healthcare Power of Attorney

If you are incapacitated, who will make decisions for you? In a healthcare power of attorney you can designate a healthcare agent (and alternates) to make healthcare decisions for you when you are unable to make them. The decisions may be critical or not. They can run from setting a broken arm to deciding whether to hook you up to a ventilator.

We used to include healthcare provisions in a financial power of attorney. Now, as our planning has improved and as life has become more complicated, we recommend that you use a separate healthcare power of attorney to lay out your wishes in detail.

The Living Will

In a living will you say what should happen if death is imminent and there's nothing more that can reasonably be done. If you are in a hospital and your doctor determines that you are terminally ill with only a short period of time to live, you can clarify that you do not want to have procedures administered that serve only to prolong the dying process. You can clarify that what is most important to you is to maintain your dignity and to be comfortable. So, for instance, if giving you pain medication might shorten your life, that's okay.

Our living will works together with our healthcare power of attorney. If the living will is clear, that's it. If there's any question about what the living will means, the person you have named in your healthcare power of attorney is authorized to clarify what you want. That way your family won't have to deal with a district judge or a hospital lawyer. Just as in the rest of your estate planning you want decisions to be made by those whom you know and trust—without a big hassle.

The HIPAA Release

In 1997 the US Congress enacted the Healthcare Information Privacy and Portability Act, now fondly known as "HIPAA," to protect the privacy of healthcare information. Like so much of what our lawmakers do, there are good parts of the law (but not as many as we hoped) and bad parts (which we didn't see coming.) Regardless, you need to deal with HIPAA in your estate planning.

HIPAA limits who can know your healthcare information. Unless you have given your okay, your healthcare providers can't share your private healthcare information—even with your family. So, for example, you have a heart attack. Your daughter immediately flies home from the East Coast. When she arrives at your hospital bed, the nurse can't tell her what's going on unless there's an authorization in your file.

In our healthcare power of attorney we include HIPAA authorizations so that your healthcare agent can find out what's going on. But you should also have a separate document stating who can know your healthcare information. No decision-making, just finding out what's going on. That's the "HIPAA release."

Healthcare Documents for your Graduate

You should also consider healthcare planning for your children or grandchildren, especially when they graduate from high school. Where will they head? If it's a college or a job far away, that raises an issue. What happens if the graduate gets in an accident or is really sick? Who back home can find out what's going on and make healthcare decisions?

Nobody! Unless the graduate signs healthcare documents before leaving home.

The graduate should sign a healthcare power of attorney to designate who can make healthcare decisions if the graduate is unable to do so. That will usually be parents.

The graduate should also sign a "HIPAA release" and perhaps a living will and a financial power of attorney.

Getting Better Health Care

As we age, we deal more and more with the health care industry. More doctor visits and tests. More hospitalizations. More medications. And more questions, confusion and stress.

So, let's discuss what you can do about it.

First, get some help: ask someone to be your "medical advocate." A medical advocate is someone who is willing and available to get involved in your health care. You let your health care providers know who this person is and you make sure they meet your providers. This person is in your corner, and you want everyone to know that. Having someone serve as a medical advocate for you can make a big difference in getting the best health care results.

Your medical advocate should accompany you on doctor visits and hospitalizations. They can help you prepare questions before appointments and make sure you ask about what is bothering you the most. If you are "out of it," they can ask the questions. When the doctor gives answers, the advocate can make sure that you both understand. And remember the doctor's answers.

That's a lot to ask someone to do for you. And not everyone can help this much. But, it's worth asking. If you can enlist your healthcare agent to be your medical advocate, I guarantee you'll get better health care.

Your Medical Records

You probably already know this, but your medical records are really yours. You're entitled to copies of everything. I suggest that you start collecting your medical records. It will probably be uncomfortable when you first start asking for copies, but get over it! It's important.

Make it a habit to get copies of the records of all your doctor visits, hospitalizations, tests, etc. Staff can either give you copies right away or send them in a few days. They'll do so if you'll just ask. Then put the records into a three-ring binder organized by health care provider. Update the binder every time you get a new document.

Now, here's where your work will pay off. Take your binder with you to your doctor visits. Then, when your doctor asks you when you first started experiencing shortness of breath, you won't have to rely on your memory. You'll be able to show your doctor the record of your medical exam in 2002 when you first started having the problem. Your doctor will be able to see what your condition was then and what the other doctor did for you. Your doctor can help you way more today when she has exact information about your symptoms, test results and the treatment that you received way back when.

Yes, maybe your doctor already has the records from your earlier exams. But there's a good chance she doesn't.

And, yes, it's not easy always asking for records, and it's a pain to organize the records and tote your notebook along with you to appointments. But isn't your health worth it?

CHAPTER 4

Dealing with Becoming Incapacitated

Guardianship and Conservatorship

What will happen if you become incapacitated? Let's say you have a stroke or you get in a bad car wreck. If you're not able to handle your affairs, what will happen?

Unless you have done proper planning beforehand, it's likely that the local court will take over, declare you legally incompetent, and appoint a guardian or conservator to serve under court supervision. This process can be lengthy, costly and stressful.

Guardianship, referred to as "conservatorship" if it involves management of an estate, is a court proceeding that places an individual, also known as a ward or protected person, under the supervision of a guardian or conservator. This is typically a family member, friend, or fiduciary who is given the authority to:

- Determine and maintain your residence
- Provide consent to and supervise your medical treatment
- Consent to and supervise non-medical services for you such as psychiatric or behavioral counseling
- Make end-of-life decisions
- Pay your debts and other expenses
- Organize, gather and protect your assets
- Manage your property and income

The guardian or conservator is required to report to the court about his or her activities on an annual basis.

Even if the court appoints the person you would have chosen, wouldn't you prefer to avoid a court becoming involved in your affairs? Wouldn't you rather decide beforehand who should handle your affairs if you become incapacitated? If so, you must designate someone in proper legal documents so that they will have the authority to act—without court involvement.

The Financial Power of Attorney and the Living Trust

Whether you base your planning on a will or a revocable living trust you will want to also prepare a financial power of attorney. We call it a durable power of attorney. This means it stays in effect if you become disabled or incapacitated, which is exactly when we want it to operate.

In a power of attorney you authorize someone and then designate backups to undertake financial transactions on your behalf. The power of attorney can be limited in scope or it can be general. In our estate planning we use general powers of attorney.

The power of attorney can be effective when you sign it or it can spring into existence upon the occurrence of an event, for instance, the certification by your attending physician that you're incapacitated. There are arguments in favor of each approach. We generally recommend a power of attorney that's immediately effective when you sign it. That way there will be no question about your agent being able to act for you down the road.

The power of attorney is only effective while you're alive, and it only gives to your agent the powers that you specify. You can revoke it whenever you wish.

We recommend that all our clients prepare a financial power of attorney. However, the power of attorney doesn't always work as well as we would wish. Financial institutions have historically been reluctant to honor them. And a power of attorney can be "trumped" by a dissatisfied family member—or other interested person—who does not like arrangements you have set up in your power of attorney and who files a guardianship or conservatorship action.

The other "legal tool" that we suggest our clients use for incapacity planning is the revocable living trust. This is a will substitute that also contains your instructions on what should happen if you become incapacitated: how to decide if you're incapacitated enough that someone else should step in and, if so, who that person should be. With a revocable living trust you should be able to avoid the shortcomings of a financial power of attorney and to avoid a guardianship or conservatorship. That means more control and privacy for you—and less expense and hassle.[1]

---

[1] We'll discuss the revocable living trust in more detail below starting at page 87.

CHAPTER 5

Long-term Care Planning

It's not "Estate Planning"

What if your health deteriorates and expensive medical and skilled nursing services eat up your estate? "Long-term care planning" allows you to protect assets if you are facing horrendous medical or nursing home expenses. People do long-term care planning so that, if Dad ends up in a nursing home, Mom doesn't have to eat cat food and there's something left to pass on to the kids when Mom and Dad are gone.

Every family should do estate planning. Some should do long-term care planning.

Who is it right for? As we lawyers love to say: "It depends." It depends on the size of the family's estate, how much income they have, and what health issues they are facing. Is there a history of dementia in the family?

Most importantly, is the family already worrying about long-term care expenses? If so, then that's enough reason to at least explore the options. They don't have to just sit back, stew about the problem and then spend all their live savings on nursing home expenses.

Because there are options. And simple wills and powers of attorney aren't going to do the trick.

A Family that Could have Benefited

One of our clients, I'll call her Mabel, waited too long. She had helped her kids all their lives. She wasn't wealthy by any means, but she enjoyed being generous with them. And one of the kids, Leigh, always needed help. Leigh had a drinking problem and couldn't hold down a job. So, Mabel paid her rent and bought her groceries and gas. She kept Leigh afloat. Mabel knew that was not how to make Leigh independent, but Mabel felt she had to help.

Then Mabel's health began to fail. She was having difficulty living alone, and her savings were being quickly depleted. She didn't want to move in with her kids. A nursing home seemed like the best place for her, but Mabel's monthly income was way less than the $7,000 to $8,000 a month that a nursing home would cost.

We in the US have a system to help people like Mabel: Medicaid. However, when Mabel and her children came in to see me, I had to tell them that Mabel's eligibility for Medicaid was going to be substantially reduced because of the gifts she had made to Leigh. Not the makings for good relations among the children. And what a sad situation for Mabel.

Ultimately, you could say Mabel and her family were lucky. They did have to use up most of her assets to pay for her care, but they were able to find an older woman who was willing to move in with Mabel and take care of her. Mabel lived for another year and a half. When she passed away, there was very little left for her children, but at least she had been able to stay home, and the other children hadn't had to pay out of their own pockets because of the gifts to Leigh. I have heard, though, that now the other children barely speak to Leigh.

I think you can see where I'm going with this. This did not need to happen. With proper long-term care planning, Mabel could have helped Leigh and still received Medicaid when she needed it.

Long-term Care Insurance

It was too late for Mabel, but the first strategy for a family to consider when they are worried about runaway nursing home expenses is long-term care insurance.

With traditional long-term care insurance you pay a premium and receive coverage if you become disabled and incur long-term care expenses. The policy kicks in when you are unable to perform two or more of the so-called "activities of daily living."

These include:

- Feeding
- Toileting
- Dressing
- Maintaining continence
- Bathing and grooming
- Walking and transferring (such as moving from bed to wheelchair)

The policy pays so much per day, perhaps $200. A good policy will have an inflation adjustment to raise this amount over time.

The policy provides payments over a fixed period of time. Typically this could be three years, five years, seven years or for your lifetime.

The other kind of long-term care coverage is through a life insurance policy with a long-term care rider. You purchase life insurance with a death benefit of, for instance, $500,000. The policy provides that, if you become disabled and begin incurring long-term care expenses, the insurance company will pay these and deduct the amount from what otherwise would be the death benefit.

Which kind of policy is better? Some people prefer the life insurance product since they know that, no matter what, they'll get something for their money. Other people say that the traditional long-term care policy is actually a better buy for most people. This is something to be sorted out with an insurance expert.

Medicaid Planning

If long-term care insurance is not a viable option, you have to use your own resources to pay for long-term care coverage until you qualify for assistance through Medicaid. Generally, Medicaid covers nursing home expenses but not assisted living facility expenses.

Medicaid covers long-term care expenses of people who qualify from a medical and from a financial standpoint. The financial requirement includes an income component and an asset component. The most important issue is usually the asset component.

Some assets, such as your home and car, are normally not counted. Countable assets must be below a certain—low—level. A single individual can't have countable assets of more than $2,000. For a couple the applicant spouse must have no more than $2,000 of countable assets and the other spouse can have assets of up to, perhaps, $120,000.

When you have made gifts within five years of your Medicaid application, like Mabel, you will be disqualified from receiving benefits for a period of time based on the value of your gifts.

If you go into a Medicaid office and ask them what to do, they are likely to tell you to spend down your assets and then come back for help. They won't mention any alternatives. But there are alternatives allowed by the law, and they are the basis of the strategies used in long-term care planning. By using these strategies your disabled family member can qualify for Medicaid and still protect a good portion of the family's assets.

Is it Ethical?

Some people object to someone planning to make himself eligible for Medicaid. It may be lawful, but they don't think it's right to try to protect some of your assets and still qualify for Medicaid. Others say that we do similar things every day, such as arranging our affairs to minimize our taxes. Is it unethical to plan your affairs so as to pay less tax than you otherwise would have or to establish entities such as corporations or limited liability companies so that, if there is a lawsuit down the road, the family can protect some of its assets? Each family must decide on its own how to think about this issue.

Veteran's Aid & Attendance

Medicaid is for all Americans who qualify for assistance. There's another benefit that is available only to wartime veterans and their spouses. It's called Veterans Aid and Attendance or sometimes the "improved pension."

The requirements for this type of assistance are similar but not identical to those of Medicaid.

The benefits are also different. Medicaid will normally not pay assisted living facility expenses but Aid and Attendance may. If you qualify for Medicaid it will pay all your unreimbursed medical expenses. Aid and Attendance has limits on how much it will pay. In 2017 they are approximately $2,120 per month for a married veteran.

For wartime veterans it often makes most sense to apply both for Medicaid and Aid and Attendance.

CHAPTER 6

Aging in Place

Where will you live as you age? That should also be part of your estate planning.

Of course, as with all estate planning, you can decide to do nothing and rely on chance. That means that someone else, probably a family member, will decide where you will live. The decision will likely be forced on them by some health event, so they will have to make decisions in a hurry, at a time of stress, and without knowing what you want.

How many times have you heard someone say something like: "I never want to end up in a nursing home. Just take me out in the backyard and shoot me." Not much guidance for the family. If they have no choice but to move you to a facility, such a comment is a sure-fire way to instill a sense of guilt that will never go away.

There is an alternative. How about getting clear in your own mind under what circumstances you would want to stay home or live elsewhere and then communicating this to your loved ones?

"Aging in Place" is a discipline that has arisen in recent years to deal with this issue. Aging in Place focuses on the ability to live in your home for as long as you want to—and as long as it is safe and comfortable to do so. I think it's such an important issue that I've taken the training to become a Certified Aging in Place Specialist.

As you think about this topic, here are some questions to consider:

- How important is it to you to stay in the family home?
- Do you want to be cared for there—no matter what and at any cost?
- How much should your family spend to keep you home? (Even those people who want to die at home often say they don't want their money to be "wasted" on a lot of medical expenses.)
- How much of a burden do you want to impose on your family to be able to keep you at home?

For you to be able to stay home the following are generally required:

- You are generally in good health.
- You have access to essential services such as home repair, housekeeping, meal preparation, lawn care and snow removal.
- You are able to drive or have access to transportation.
- You live in a home that can be safe and comfortable.

If you conclude that you can stay home, Aging in Place planning then focuses on your home. How well does it work for you right now? How would it work if you were confined to a wheelchair? What would it cost to do the remodeling necessary to accommodate that situation?

There are many modifications that can be made to the home to make it more appropriate as you age. They start with changing the light switches and knobs on doors and cupboards and extend to remodeling the entrance to the home and the bathroom so that it is wheelchair-accessible.

If you decide that your present home isn't the best place for you, you'll then want to consider other options. Another home, a condo, an independent living facility or an assisted living facility? Each alternative has its pros and cons.

To Die at Home

Where would you want to spend your last days if you suffer a stroke or have some other medical condition that has confined you to bed and given you a short life expectancy?

If possible, would you want to be at home, or are you fine with being in a facility like a nursing home or a hospice? For myself, when I come to the end of my days, if at all possible I'd like to die at home.

Whether I can do so will depend on my physical condition and my financial condition: can I afford to pay for in-home care? But it will also depend on whether I've done planning ahead of time to make it happen.

Let me share a story that has really bothered me. One of my farmer clients, let's call him Dale, was in his eighties. Dale was very successful. He had a big, debt-free farm and a loving family. He was a little hard of hearing, but otherwise his health was pretty good. He was sharp and fun to talk to.

Then one day he had a stroke and ended up in a nursing home. He hated it, especially the constant noise and lack of privacy. He wanted to go home. But, despite his millions, he couldn't. And I couldn't do anything about it. We had done his basic estate planning, but it didn't help.

At that point Dale had lost control of his life. Others—his healthcare professionals and his family—had assumed control. That's exactly what Dale had thought should happen if he became disabled when we did his estate planning. And they wanted to do what was best for him.

The healthcare professionals told the family that the nursing home was the best place for Dale. (And, anyway, that is where "everyone" who needs a high level of care ends up, isn't it?)

And it takes a lot of work—and money—to get a family home set up to take care of an invalid. Handicap-accessible bathroom, hand rails, a hospital bed. Home healthcare people. Where do you even find someone to do such work, especially when the home is on a farm? There are a lot of moving parts. What would it cost?

So, Dale's family never seriously considered doing what Dale told them he wanted as he lay in the nursing home bed. Even though there was plenty of money to pay for twenty-four hour care and to retrofit the home for his care.

The lawyer in me has to point out that the heirs were in a conflict of interest situation: every extra dollar spent on Dale's healthcare reduced their inheritance by a dollar. But I don't want to point fingers. Except at Dale—and myself.

Dale couldn't die at home because he had not done the planning ahead of time—while he was still in control. When we were doing Dale's estate planning, he said that he didn't want his money to be "wasted" on a lot of medical expenses. But I wish I had prodded him. I'll bet he also would have said that he would like to die at home if he could—and that it was okay to use part of his ample estate for that. If we had put a specific plan in place and he had discussed it with the family, I'm sure they would have agreed and followed his wishes. The kids could probably have gotten by with an inheritance of $7.9 million instead of $8 million.

Not everyone will have the same viewpoint, and many won't have the financial means to die at home if that is medically possible. What about you?

CHAPTER 7

Who Should Handle Your Affairs?

Healthcare Agents

Now let's consider whom you want to name to help if you become incapacitated or pass away. That means making healthcare decisions for you if you can't and handling your affairs if you're incapacitated or gone. Besides administering your estate it may mean helping your heirs manage their inheritance. If you have minor children, it means designating a guardian if you and your spouse are both gone.

Healthcare decisions are often time-sensitive. So, you may name a partner or spouse as primary decision-maker and then someone who lives nearby as a backup. People often want to name their kids as backups, which may be fine unless they live across the country.

You may decide that there are several people who could serve as backup healthcare decision-makers and that you'd be comfortable with any of them acting alone. If so, you might designate, say, all three of your kids "individually or jointly," meaning that if only one can make it to the hospital in time to help, he can act alone. But if there's time for all three kids to come, you want them to all participate in the decision-making.

Agents to Handle your Finances

When it comes to handling financial affairs, most people provide that their spouses or partners will be trustees of the trusts or personal representative of the wills they establish. But, if the spouse can't serve, who will? This is one of the most difficult issues for many clients—and one of the biggest sources of family fights.

Generally, trustees can be family members, friends, accountants, lawyers and professional trust companies. You can name more than one trustee. There are advantages and disadvantages to each possible arrangement.

Serving as trustee is a real job, not just an honorary title. The trustee must understand and follow the directions in the trust agreement and the law generally. The trustee must manage and account for all trust assets, as well as file necessary tax returns. A trustee is a "fiduciary" under the law. This means that the trustee has a high level of responsibility to carry out his or her duties in good faith and with honesty. The trustee must avoid self-dealing or conflicts of interest in which the potential benefit to the fiduciary is in conflict with what is best for the trust beneficiaries. The best interest of the beneficiaries must be primary, and absolute candor is required of the fiduciary.

Many people are inclined to name family members as trustees. Perhaps the oldest child or, if he can't serve, the middle child. Maybe two of the children. This is all right, but is the child really up to the job? Will he or she have the time and interest to fulfill the trustee's role? Do the kids really get along that well?

Sometimes it makes sense to name a family member and either a CPA or a trust company as co-trustees. That way the family member can bring knowledge of the family into the equation, and the other trustee can focus on the business and compliance issues.

Corporate trustees are in the business of managing trusts. They have competent, dependable employees and processes in place. They manage assets in a conservative manner and are careful to follow the directions in the trust agreement. The downside of corporate trustees is that they generally charge more for their services than other trustees would.

A Father Who Named the Wrong Agent

A lawyer friend tells of a farmer who died leaving a son and daughter. His living trust directed that the trustee distribute his trust estate, including his farm, to his son. He left investments equal to 10% of his estate in "TOD" (transfer on death) accounts for his daughter. He named the daughter as trustee and personal representative of his will. When the farmer died, he had his farm in trust, and he had the TOD accounts and $60,000 in assets in his sole name (not in trust or in TOD accounts).

So, what happened?

The daughter collected her TOD accounts. She filed the will to get herself appointed as personal representative.

Then she just sat. For five years.

Basically, all she had to do was transfer the $60,000 of assets into the trust and distribute the trust assets to her brother. But she wouldn't do anything.

Her brother—and his lawyers—went to court time and again, but they couldn't get the judge to make her do her job or fire her. Finally there was a trial, and the judge settled the estate.

I don't know if the father explained to his daughter why he was leaving her such a small part of his estate. I'm guessing he didn't.

I don't know why he named his daughter to handle his affairs when he gave his son the lion's share of his estate. Did he feel that he was evening things out by giving her the job of administering his estate? Obviously the daughter didn't see things that way.

I don't know why the farmer's advisors didn't help him make better decisions and get his trust funded.

And I don't know what the brother and sister's relationship was before dad died. But I know what it was after the trial.

What a sad story—and what an example of bad planning.

Naming a Guardian for your Minor Children

If you have minor children, the toughest decision may be whom to name as guardian for the children if something happens to you and your spouse.

The thought of somebody else raising your children is hard enough, but there are so many factors to consider. Who would have the time, the energy and the ability to take on the children? Would the children have to move to an unfamiliar community? Most importantly, would the guardian share your values and raise your children as you'd want them to be raised?

The person whom you name is not bound to accept the appointment, and a judge could override your nomination in unusual circumstances, but your decision will usually stand. Generally, you will name one person or perhaps a couple. Of course, you'll want to name backups if the people you name can't serve.

It's a tough decision, but if you don't make it, a judge who has never met the family—or the proposed guardian—will make it for you. So, you may not be sure about your decision, but it's certainly better than a stranger's.

CHAPTER 8

Who Gets What?

Your Spouse or Partner Usually Comes First

Passing on your financial legacy means leaving your property to whom you want, when you want and the way you want. Let's consider some of the issues you may want to address as you think about this goal.

First, some priorities. You may have the greatest kids in the world, but if you're married or have a significant other, he or she usually comes first. In other words, if something happens to you, your first priority is to take care of your partner, right? That's what most of us think, anyway.

So, what will you leave your partner? If you're lucky enough to have a large estate, you may decide that your partner can do fine without receiving all of your estate and that you can leave something to the kids or grandkids even if you predecease your partner.

That leads us to second marriages. If you have kids from a prior marriage, how certain can you be that your new partner will take care of them if you predecease him or her? We've seen way too many cases where the kids from a first marriage come out on the short end.

And, what if your surviving spouse remarries after you're gone? If you're like most people you'd still want your spouse to benefit from your estate, but you wouldn't want your spouse's new partner—or his or her family—to end up with your property.

Leaving Property Outright or in Trust

If you leave property to your spouse or partner outright, that means there are no strings attached. If he or she wants to sell it, give it away or just ignore it, that's up to him or her.

What if the husband has planned for his grandson to take over the ranch—like my great grandfather did—but he doesn't address the issue in his planning, he just leaves everything outright to his wife? Then, the widow, just like my great grandmother, can do whatever she wants to—or whatever some family member or friend convinces her to do, like booting her grandson off the place.

Leaving property outright also means that, if the surviving spouse has a problem with creditors, the inheritance will be subject to the creditor's claims. What kind of creditors? Well, if your spouse keeps driving after she should really quit, it may be the plaintiff's lawyer representing the people whom your spouse hits when she goes through a red light. (Yes, I know she should have liability insurance, but how good will she be about paying all her bills, like insurance statements, when she gets to that point?)

Another factor to consider is how well your surviving spouse or partner will be able to manage the assets you leave them. Many people have let their spouses handle all the finances and are in the dark when they're left alone to manage everything.

There's also a tax angle to how you leave property to your spouse. Some trust arrangements can save a lot of estate tax and/or income tax. But they are more complicated and expensive to implement than an outright gift or bequest. So, you'll have to balance how important it is to have simplicity versus tax minimization.[2]

---

[2] We discuss many of the tax issues below in Chapter 16.

Leaving Assets to your Spouse or Partner in Trust

Let's say you decide that it does make sense to leave property in trust. If so, you have a lot of discretion in setting up the arrangements. Clients are often amazed at what we can do with careful trust planning. This is where your team of advisors can help you sort out the options and come up with a plan that you thoroughly understand and that fits the specific circumstances of your family.

You may let the spouse serve as trustee, managing the assets, paying himself or herself in accordance with your instructions. But you'll include instructions on what to do—and who should step in—if your spouse can't manage the job.

Most of our clients provide that the surviving spouse can have all the income earned by the assets in the trust and, if need be, the survivor can have access to some or all of the principal. When the surviving spouse passes away, the trust specifies who is to receive what is left, usually kids or grandkids.

Leaving property in trust allows your surviving spouse to be well taken care of but also allows you to make sure the property ends up passing in accordance with your plans. I often wonder how different my life would have been if my great grandfather had documented his plans with my dad. I really enjoy working as an attorney, but farmers get to wear baseball caps instead of bowties.

No one, I guess, has a plan to remarry if their spouse passes away. When I'm helping clients design their estate plans, I'll raise the topic of the surviving spouse remarrying. Generally my clients scoff at the idea, and we joke about it. But the more that they think about it, the more they realize it could happen. Usually they have heard at least one story of an elderly person marrying or becoming romantically involved with someone. If not, I ask them to Google "nursing home romance."

I then explain how I suggest dealing with the issue through a "remarriage provision." This part of the trust says, in effect, that, if the surviving spouse wants to get remarried later on, that's fine. We want him or her to be happy. But we don't want some stranger to end up with our property. So the surviving spouse must enter into a premarital agreement to continue benefiting from the trust.

CHAPTER 9

Leaving Property
to Other Family Members

Once you have provided for your spouse or partner, who comes next? Usually it's other family members, kids and perhaps grandkids or nephews or nieces. It may be other family members or friends who are facing a disability or other serious problem and will need help down the road.[3]

If we're dealing with children, will we treat them the same, regardless of how well each has done? This can be a big factor in avoiding hurt feelings and bad family relations. When there's even a slight discrepancy between what the kids get, I've seen great unhappiness and finger-pointing among the children.

Even if you'd like to treat the kids equally, it may not make sense in your family if you have one asset that comprises a big part of your estate. In my practice it's often a family farm or ranch. As we help clients sort through their priorities, they come to the realization that it's more important to them to keep the farm in the

---

[3] Parents sometimes think they must disinherit their disabled child in order to preserve his or her Supplemental Security Income/Medicaid benefits. Not true. You can leave property in a "Special Needs Trust" that preserves assets for the benefit of the disabled person while allowing them to continue receiving government benefits. That way you can provide for the child in ways not provided by the government programs.

.

family than to treat their kids equally. Particularly if one child has been working in the business for a long time, many parents decide that it's just fair to give that child more of the farm or business. What to do with a family business is worth its own chapter. See Chapter 11, page 69.

Leaving Too Much

Many of our clients have what at first blush seems like an easy problem. They have a very large estate. That's great, but what if they leave "too much" to their children? They don't want to create trust fund babies who don't feel a need to contribute and just waste their lives living off their inheritance.

How much is too much? That's a difficult question to answer. As in so much of estate planning, there's no "right" answer. All we can do is to discuss and think through these issues. Generally our clients have never really talked about these issues together. There's a lot of emotion in these discussions. Having a third party to ask good questions and to keep the discussion moving in a positive direction can be crucial. Many parents decide that part of the answer is to structure the inheritance to pay out over time or to base payouts on what the child himself earns.

Leaving Property to Grandkids

Maybe you have grandchildren. Do you want to leave part of your estate to them? Many clients just leave their estates to their children, feeling that the children can take care of the grandkids. There are risks to this, as when you leave property outright to a child who isn't good with money, so some clients leave specific distributions to grandchildren. For clients whose estates will likely generate estate tax, it can be advantageous tax-wise to skip a generation and leave property directly to the grandchildren.[4] This makes sense if your kids will do fine without receiving all of your estate.

And you may want to focus more on "the big picture." As you think about your life and the family you leave behind, would you want to benefit as many generations as you reasonably can? You can't control what happens five generations down the line, probably, but you can have a big effect not only on your children but on your grandchildren.

It costs a lot of money to go to Harvard. If your granddaughter can get in, would you want to help her financially? And, if your grandson wants to start a business, that's going to take some capital. Would you want to leave some seed capital to help him get started? Certainly your children can help their own kids, but your providing for your grandchildren may make a big difference in their lives.

When Would You Want to Leave Property in Trust?

Just as with leaving property to your spouse or partner, you can either leave assets to kids or grandkids outright or in trust where you specify who should manage the property and how distributions should be handled.

Here are some of the questions to ask yourself as you weigh the options:

1. Can the heir competently manage the property?

You will want to consider the heir's age, whether he or she has any problems, such as disabilities or problems with alcohol or drugs, and what experience the heir has managing assets like the ones you plan to give him or her.

---

[4] Uncle Sam knows this and has a special tax, the "generation-skipping transfer tax," to deal with this strategy, but this tax has a large exemption that families can take advantage of.

If the heir is a minor, it's an easy decision. You don't want to leave a 14 year-old $100,000 in cash. You'll want to name a responsible person to serve as trustee to manage the property and pay the reasonable expenses of the beneficiary. You specify what expenses. Normally you'll want the trust to cover living expenses and medical and educational expenses.

If the heir is an adult, the amount involved is an important factor. It's one thing to leave a $1,000 bequest outright but quite another thing to leave $1,000,000 to someone who has never dealt with such a large amount.

If the heir is incompetent or has a drug or alcohol problem, it's the same answer. You know they won't be good managers of their inheritance, so it makes sense to leave their inheritance to them so that they can enjoy the property but not fritter it away.

2. Are you concerned about protecting the property from the heir's creditors?

Does the beneficiary have any creditor problems or do you foresee some creditor problems? If so, don't you want your inheritance to benefit the heir instead of a creditor or plaintiff's lawyer?

Lawsuits are a feature of modern life that we can philosophize about all day long, but they are something to be reckoned with. Your son sells a piece of property thinking all is well and then later is sued when it doesn't meet with the buyer's satisfaction because of some condition your son wasn't even aware of. Or, he's in a car wreck and someone is hurt. He thought he had plenty of insurance coverage but the claim vastly exceeds his insurance coverage. Or, he's in business with someone who he thought would be a perfect partner but who turns out not to be.

Is the beneficiary in a marriage that looks rocky? If your beneficiary divorces, most people want the inheritance to benefit the beneficiary and his or her descendants, not an ex-spouse.

The law of divorces is a subject for another day, but judges are generally given an incredible amount of discretion to award property between two divorcing spouses, regardless of where the property came from. We hope and expect that the judge would award property to the spouse who had inherited it or received it as a gift from his or her parents. But the law tells the judge that where property came from is only one factor to be considered in distributing assets between divorcing parties.

3. Are you concerned about what would happen if the heir dies prematurely?

If you leave property to your daughter and she dies before your son-in-law, how important is it that your inheritance benefits your grandchildren instead of your son-in-law's new wife and family?

4. How concerned are you about minimizing taxes?

Taxes are also worth their own chapter. See Chapter 17 below.

CHAPTER 10

Dealing with Specific Assets

Do you have a special asset that you'd like to leave to a specific person? It might be something as big as the family cabin, or it might be Grandma Shirley's china.

Dealing with these assets, even if their main value is only sentimental, can be an important aspect of your planning. Taking the time to sort out the issues—and then to clearly document your decisions— can avoid a lot of hurt feelings and be a huge benefit to the family.

That means preparing a document stating your wishes, not relying on oral comments or "yellow stickies" attached to the back of the picture that is to go to Bobby. You don't want a situation to arise after you're gone where it looks like some of the stickies have been moved, and some are gone. And where your spouse told three of the kids they could all have the same antique table. Families have not spoken for twenty years over such issues. Just as many family fights have erupted over who gets dad's 30-30 rifle as who gets the farm.[5]

---

[5] Passing guns to the next generation presents special issues because of federal and state restrictions on transfer.

    Certain types of guns are subject to particularly strict regulations. But all guns are subject to procedural requirements on transfer and limitations on taking or sending them to a state where it is prohibited, or giving them to a person who is legally prohibited from owning them. Some people cannot possess firearms. This includes anyone who was ever convicted of a felony or of misdemeanor domestic violence, is prohibited by a restraining order from harassing an intimate partner, uses a controlled substance unlawfully, or is an illegal alien.

    You and your estate representatives need to be aware of these rules.

Oh, and what about pets? Even though your pet is part of the family, it's also an "asset" that you should consider in your planning. A number of my clients have designated who should get their pets and set aside a fund for their care. I think that's great, but I don't think you need to get as far are Leona Helmsley, the New York hotel tycoon. Do you remember her? She left 10 million dollars for her pet dog. (A judge later reduced the amount to "only" three million.)

Hopefully, family members can take care of your pet without your making any formal arrangements. If not, and if you are concerned that your pet will just end up in the pound when you're gone, you may want to establish a "pet trust." You can name someone to manage funds that you designate to provide for your pet's care. Then, when the pet has died, the pet trust can terminate and the remaining trust property can be distributed as you direct.

The Family Cabin

What to do with the family cabin is a major planning issue for those of us out West. For those in New England it might be a cottage, and wherever you are it might be a special boat or condo. It has often been in the family for generations, and it's is an important part of the legacy to pass to the kids and grandkids.

People will start the planning discussion by stating that they want a plan that will guarantee that the cherished asset is never sold. As we discuss the issues, though, our clients often recognize that it is not realistic or even desirable to prohibit the kids from selling the asset if things don't work out. It's one thing for the family to enjoy the cabin when Mom and Dad are still around to handle the arrangements, deal with the inevitable squabbles—and pay the bills! It's another thing when the kids are in charge.

Let's say you've had a cabin for many years that all the kids enjoy. But your daughter in Delaware rarely makes it home. Why should she pay as much as your son who goes to the cabin every weekend? What about the grandkids who trash the place and leave it for others to clean up? And who's going to pay for the new roof that the cabin has needed for so long? As you think about it, don't you agree that the last thing you would want is for problems with the cabin to tear the family apart?

So, it's worth taking the time to discuss the specifics. Who will likely use the cabin, what expenses will there be and how will they be paid? We don't want to saddle the kids with property they can't afford.

Once you have reviewed these issues you may decide to simply leave the cabin to one or more of the kids with no further instructions. Or you may decide to transfer the cabin to one or more kids right away, while you are still around. That may be a good strategy, but it does raise a tax issue.[6]

If you decide that your family will likely be able to keep the cabin in the family well into the future, you may want to set up a legal ownership structure so that, when the kids inherit, there are already arrangements in place to deal with decision-making, such as how to "split the sheets" with the least acrimony and expense if it doesn't work as planned.

Under this arrangement, if one of the kids wants to get cashed out, it's already been decided how to handle the issue. Usually that means he or she will be paid, but not top dollar and not in cash. Instead,

---

[6] If Mom and Dad have a large enough estate to be facing estate taxes, transferring the cabin sooner rather than later may save estate taxes. If the family does not face estate tax, mom and dad can save the kids capital gains tax by transferring the cabin at their deaths and not during their lifetimes. Then, if the kids sell the cabin, they'll pay less tax because of the "step-up" in income tax basis that assets receive on death.

there will be payment arrangements that give those family members who want to keep the cabin a fighting chance to pay off the debt without having to sell the cabin. Part of this planning may include establishing a "slush fund" to pay cabin bills for at least a few years.

Philanthropy

Many people want to share their wealth with others beyond their immediate family. Whether that means charities or just extended family members or friends, it's what I consider philanthropy.

Through philanthropy you promote your legacy. It allows you to express what is important to you and how you want to be remembered. That might be educational opportunity or the advancement of knowledge or freedom. It could be the alleviation of suffering, eradication of disease or protecting our environment. For some it may mean protecting grizzly bears, but let's leave that discussion for another day!

Philanthropy can also function as a way to "grow" your children and grandchildren as stewards of wealth and citizens of our communities. If you establish a family foundation and name your kids to the board, you are providing them an opportunity to learn about money management, how to work as part of the team—and to expand their own horizons about what is important in life. So, your philanthropy leaves a legacy of meaning in addition to family wealth.

Who might be the recipients of your philanthropy? Of course, charities are likely candidates. How has your community experience affected your life? Think of the organizations, causes or issues that you have found especially meaningful. How would you like members of your community to remember you?

Philanthropy can also extend to helping individuals directly. Was Uncle Dick always there for you as a teenager to help you sort through difficult issues and give you some perspective? Now that's he's homebound, a ramp for his front door might make a lot of difference to him. Did the seed money that Aunt Edith gave you to get started in your business make a huge difference to your future? With the downturn in the market and as a result of some poor financial advice, she's having a hard time making ends meet now. And, would you like to help Cousin Jill as she struggles with the multiple sclerosis that has already caused her so many difficulties?

Philanthropy can also just be about making sure your employees are well taken care of when you sell your business. I have dealt with many business owners transitioning out of their business who have put arrangements in place for their longtime employees, even though it meant the owners received less for the sale of their business.

Of course, with charitable planning as with all estate planning there is a tax angle. A donation to charity is income tax deductible. But we can do even better than that with charitable planning tools such as the charitable remainder trust. This tool allows you to give to charity while also providing tax-advantaged, secure financial support for you and your family.

We used a charitable remainder trust for one of our client families who had an estate of approximately $3,000,000, half of which was made up of rental properties. The clients wanted to start selling the properties since they could no longer manage them, but they had purchased the properties many years earlier and had depreciated them so that their income tax basis was very low. That meant that, if they sold the properties, they could pay a lot of income tax.

These clients wanted their estate to benefit their children, but they also wanted to give substantial gifts to charity. Theirs was a classic case where a charitable remainder trust could accomplish their purposes—including saving taxes.

We set up a charitable remainder trust and transferred their rental properties to the trust. The trust then sold the properties and used the proceeds to make regular payments to family members. We designed the trust to pay the clients income equal to 7% of the trust balance each year during their lives. Upon the death of the survivor the remainder will go to their designated charities. (Even though the trust is irrevocable the clients can change the charitable beneficiaries.)

Here's the power of this approach: if our clients had sold their rental properties themselves, they would have had to pay income tax on the gain right away, so they would only have had the reduced, after-tax proceeds to invest. But when the charitable remainder trust sold properties, no income tax was immediately due. We were able to defer the tax by paying it in installments as payments are made through the years to the family beneficiaries. This is the same kind of tax deferral that makes IRAs so popular.

But wait! There's more! With a charitable remainder trust the clients were also entitled to a current charitable income tax deduction equal to the value of the charities' remainder.

CHAPTER 11

The Family Business

Many of our clients own businesses, whether in town or in the country. They have worked hard and managed their business well. But they have often done nothing to plan for the future of their business.

Only thirty percent of businesses successfully pass to the second generation, and only fifteen percent pass to the third generation. There may be business reasons for this failure, such as insufficient capital, but the most important reason for these sad statistics is the failure to plan.

Most business owners want to pass their estate on to their children and to treat the children all the same. But for many business owners—especially farmers and ranchers—an overriding goal is to keep the business in the family. Usually the business is the biggest family asset, and the family is asset rich and cash poor. If one child has stepped into the business, how do you allow him or her to keep the farm but still take care of the off-farm heirs? If you leave the family business to all the kids, your daughter in Seattle may end up telling your son in the business exactly what he needs to do, and demanding a regular dividend. What if there is no cash to pay them?

Transitioning the business can raise some difficult issues. Dad doesn't want to let go of control. He doesn't think Junior or the other employees can manage the business. The likely successors don't have enough money to buy out Mom and Dad. The two kids who work in the business seem to get along fine while Dad is still around, but how about after Dad is gone?

This situation requires some tough choices to be made. First, does it really make sense to keep the business? If so, how can you provide a "fair" share to the kids who aren't directly involved? If you decide the son on the place has to pay something to his sister in Seattle to even things out, what can he afford to pay, and how can we structure the payments so he can deal with drought years and low commodity prices? If the only way to make the plan work is to include non-farm heirs in farm ownership, how can we give the farmer the authority he needs to run the farm—and the proper compensation for his hard work—while allowing the non-farm heirs to eventually benefit from their inheritance?

We address these issues when working with our clients on their estate planning, and the results of our work are found in their wills or trusts. We also suggest our clients do additional planning focused on the business itself. You may have heard of such planning as "business succession" or "business exit" planning.

Our Process for business succession planning

To introduce you to this type of planning, let me describe our process for business succession planning, The Business Succession Solution. We break down the job into seven steps:

1. *The Goal Refiner*—where we help you define your goals.

2. *The Business Value Estimator*—where we determine business value and discretionary cash flow.

3. *The Growth Game Plan*—where we focus on making the business as profitable and salable as possible before transition.

4. *The Insider Transition Planner*—where we analyze how purchase by a child or employee could be structured.

5. *The Third Party Sale Planner*—where we analyze how purchase by a third party could work.

6. *The Continuity Guarantee*—where we plan for an untimely death or disability.

7. *The Plan Integrator*—where we make sure your personal estate planning supports your business succession planning.

Step 1: Defining Goals

We start in *The Goal Refiner* to not only identify but to prioritize what you want to accomplish. How long do you want to stay active in the business? Who would you like to take over if possible? How much after-tax income will you need from the business to be able to retire comfortably given your resources other than the business?

Business owners often have other goals as well. You may have long-term employees whom you want to take care of. You may want to see the business grow to the next stage.

You've probably already thought about many of the issues, but not in a structured way. Usually, you haven't prioritized your goals— or even recognized that some of the goals are inconsistent with other goals. And, very commonly you haven't discussed the issues with the other people who will be involved in the transition. So, this stage of the planning process is very valuable.

Step 2: Determining Value

Before we get too far into the planning, we need to focus on economic reality. In *The Business Value Estimator* we look at what the business is really worth. We want your planning to be realistic, and business owners often don't know how much the business is worth.

Then, what kind of cash flow does the business generate? The most likely purchaser of the business is often an "insider," an employee or a child. They may make great successors, but there's just one problem: they don't have any money! The business needs to be able to cover its expenses and put aside money for capital improvements. Then, if there's money left over, "discretionary cash flow," this can be used to pay you. So, we need to get a good handle on the discretionary cash flow early on in our planning.

Step 3: Making the Business as Salable as Possible

The Growth Game Plan: Once you have 1) clarified your goals, 2) figured out what your business is worth, and 3) determined how much cash flow it generates that could fund a sale, we focus on putting things in place today to make the transition successful.

We start with what you can do before the transition to grow the business, to make it more viable and salable. How can you grow cash flow and make it predictable? Is there some income tax planning we can do to increase profitability? This is when your accountant will lead the charge. And what can we do to protect the company's assets?

Restructuring the Business Using Entities

When business owners want to leave property to their kids or to sell the business to kids or employees, we often recommend that the owners set up an ownership structure that will be in place for the transition.

You want to make sure ownership stays in the family and to make sure you can still control the business without interference, even though you now have junior partners. If you expect your estate to be large enough to face estate taxes, making gifts of partial interests in an entity could end up saving the family estate taxes after you're gone.

The preferred entity is often a limited liability company. When we establish an LLC, we hold off transferring any interests in the LLC until we have prepared an operating agreement. That way, we have arrangements in place to stay in control and to deal with the most common problems that arise with new owners beforehand.

The toughest issue is often what to do when the new arrangement hasn't worked out for whatever reason and the new owner needs to be bought out. The LLC operating agreement will have the answers we need to treat people fairly and minimize problems for those remaining in the business. So, for instance, we don't want any dispute about the price, so there will be a mechanism to set the price. It will be fair but likely not on the high side. Perhaps there will be a discount from appraised value. After all, there won't be a realtor's commission.

We don't want to create a cash flow problem for the business, so the operating agreement will provide for payments to the departing owner over time with interest and at a modest but fair rate paid on the balance.

With the LLC operating agreement you make all these decisions ahead of time, so that you can start transferring ownership in the way that makes the most sense without the fear of losing control or of exacerbating disputes down the road.

Often a business's most important assets are its employees. If that's true in your business, our planning may involve preparing "golden handcuffs" to tie the key employees to the company, making it too good a deal to stay with the company rather than going across the street. That may include a written agreement with the employee to protect the confidentiality of the information he or she will obtain, such as customer lists.

If you plan to sell to a third party, we know they and their advisors will do "due diligence" on the business, looking closely at all aspects of the operation. What can we do ahead of time to prepare for that review? How are the corporate books? Is the accounting system what it should be?

This step of our process often also involves figuring out how to "grow" the buyers into owners. This is valuable because, although the likely buyers may be very good at their jobs, they often have no idea what it means to run the business as an owner. There is a big difference between the skills and mindset of an employee and those of an owner. Training a successor may be the most important thing the business owner can do to make a transition successful.

This "growing" the buyers is challenging, and the toughest part is often getting Dad to sit down with the successor on a regular basis and pass on the information the successor will need to run the company. This can include:

1. What the most important financial and operational metrics for the business are;

2. How to read the company's financial statements;

3. How and when to get help from the company's advisors, and, of course,

4. How to deal with the company's customers, vendors, employees—and bankers.

The business owner has never shared this information with anyone. Lots of follow-up by the advisors is usually needed here!

Steps 4 and 5: Insider or Third-Party Sale Planning

Steps four and five of our business succession process, *The Insider Transition Planner* and *The Third Party Sale Planner*, deal with planning for purchase either by an insider or an outsider. After identifying likely successors, we start figuring out what structure of deal would work best.

If you are going to sell your business the most likely buyer is an insider. What can you start putting in place now so that the sale can actually take place as planned? Since these buyers rarely have money, in Step Four we work on structuring a sale where the buyer can use the money earned by the business itself to finance the purchase. The important issue here is to make sure you, the seller, are protected. That means not turning over control until you have been paid and structuring payment so that you're not strung out too long.

We start with the proposition that the buyer must have some "skin in the game." They should put up a down payment. If it means they have to borrow against their home, so be it.

We then revisit our analysis of the business's cash flow. After allowing for expenses, taxes and capital expenditures how much will be available to pay off the remaining purchase? If we capitalize this projected stream of cash, how long will it take to pay off the principal balance? We don't want you waiting for twenty years to get paid off!

Many of the transactions we have helped structure involve a two-step process. Initially the business owner sells a minority interest to the employees or family members. The seller will usually finance this part of the deal himself. This step may take five years. During this time the seller works with the buyer to teach him the ropes, to "grow him into an owner." Then as the second step in the process the buyer—who now owns, say, 40% of the business outright and knows how to run the business—borrows the remaining sales price from a bank to pay off the seller. Thus, the seller gets paid off in perhaps six years—and not twenty.

Sometimes the plan involves gifting some or all of the business to children. If so, you will still want to consider control issues and tax issues. If you don't already operate through a corporation or an LLC you may want to form one so that you can then gift minority interests to your children over time, as I discussed above. If you decide the most likely buyer is a third party, we want to anticipate their likely concerns and requirements and to prepare to meet them. If you have a business that may attract a third-party buyer, you can avoid or at least minimize owner financing. A third-party buyer will likely have cash to invest.

Our planning will include figuring out what we can do to attract qualified buyers, how much you, the seller, are willing to finance yourself and what involvement you are willing to maintain with the business after closing.

Step 6: If An Owner dies during the Transition

The Continuity Guarantee, Step Six in our process, involves what I call business continuity planning. What happens if we have a plan to transition the business in five years and the owner dies in year three? It's easy to picture what would happen without planning. Key employees loyally attend the owner's funeral on Monday. But they are sending out their resumes on Tuesday! If key employees leave, the family will be left with a business that might be sold for pennies on the dollar.

We might address the issue of key employees jumping ship by instituting a "stay bonus" program. The Company buys life insurance with a death benefit large enough to pay key employees' salaries—plus a substantial bonus—for one to two years. We then tell the key employees that, if something happens to the owner, there will be enough to pay them their normal salaries plus a bonus of, perhaps, 50%, to be paid every 90 days as long as the employee stays with the Company.

Thus, the key employees know the Company has money to pay their salaries, and they know they can earn a big bonus if they stay during a transition period. They may leave after a new owner takes over, but they'll remain long enough to give the deceased business owner's family some breathing room to arrange a sale—and not at a fire sale price.

An equally important issue covered in this stage of our planning is what happens when a co-owner dies, becomes disabled or just wants to leave the Company. We want to make sure that there is an agreement among the owners that will protect everyone. This is either a partnership agreement, the LLC operating agreement discussed above or, if the business is a corporation, it's a shareholders' agreement, which is often called a buy/sell agreement. It will deal with the situation when one of the owners dies, becomes disabled, wants to sell out, gets fired or wants to quit. The agreement can provide a mechanism to set a fair value for an owner's interest and provide reasonable payment terms for buyout.

If the agreement calls for life insurance to fund a buyout upon death, we will want to make sure there actually is a policy with an appropriate death benefit—payable to the appropriate person. (With older agreements that haven't been reviewed we often find that the death benefit is based on what the company was worth 20 years ago and that the death benefits are not payable as they should be.)

Step 7: Coordination with Personal Estate Planning

Finally, in the last step of the business succession process, *The Plan Integrator*, we look at your personal estate planning. It needs to be coordinated with your business succession planning, of course. Very often we find that the business owner hasn't done the kind of personal estate planning that will accomplish his or her goals, so we update the estate planning while we're working on the business succession plan.

CHAPTER 12

Lifetime Gifts

The First Priority

Estate planning obviously involves transferring property when someone dies. But it can also involve lifetime transfers. If you already know who you want to receive your property, you might just transfer it now. As we'll discuss, there may be good reasons to do so. But, as in all planning we need to base decisions on your priorities and goals.

In estate planning the first priority is to take care of Mom and Dad. Yes, you love your children and want to take care of them. And, yes, you want to minimize taxes. But you're not gone yet! So, you should base your planning on making sure you can live out your lives in comfort and security. That takes precedence over just focusing on transferring the most property possible to the kids. That means that, before you start making big gifts during your lifetime, you have made sure you'll be left with enough to feel financially secure.

If you decide that you can indeed afford to transfer some of your property during your lifetime, the next question is: does it make sense from the standpoint of the recipient? Does the intended recipient want or need the gift? If you gift it to him or her, will it just be wasted? Will it end up doing more harm than good for the recipient? (Think "trust fund baby.")

You will then want to decide whether to gift the property outright or in trust. The same factors as to how you should leave property to family members as we discussed concerning transfers at death are applicable to lifetime gifts. If you want to transfer property to a family member but feel they're not able to properly manage the property, you can gift the property in trust (see the discussion on page 59 above.)

There also can be a tax angle to lifetime gifts. I discuss this in Chapter 17 on taxes.

CHAPTER 13

Keeping Things Simple

If you have worked your way through the issues laid out above you have a pretty good idea of what your estate planning should accomplish. Now, what about documenting your wishes? We all want to keep things simple. What does that mean for your estate planning?

What it <u>doesn't</u> mean is short documents with no detail. Simple means easy to understand exactly what you want to happen and easy to make that happen. That way, if you're not able to say what you want, we can look at your planning documents for your instructions. We don't have to go ask some judge what he thinks should happen to you or your property.

Simple Planning for a Farm Family

I learned this lesson when working with a large farming family.

Mom and Dad had a wonderful farm and a half dozen kids, so they wisely decided to do some estate planning. They went to an attorney who drafted wills where each spouse left his or her share of their estate to the survivor in trust. Whether this lawyer was a believer in short documents or the clients insisted on short documents I don't know, but the wills contained only a few sentences on how the trust was to work.

Dad died shortly afterwards, and Mom inherited his half of the estate through the trust that he'd left her. All went well until Mom developed dementia and the kids started squabbling about what to do with the farm. All but one of the kids thought that the farm should be sold, but one demanded it should be kept. That's when I got involved.

The problem? The trust agreement had no instructions on whether the trustees were authorized to sell the farm. We therefore had to go to court to have a judge decide if the trustees should be allowed to sell the farm. To make our case to the judge we turned to Montana law, but there was no Montana legal authority that dealt with the question. So we ended up trying to find the answer in the law from jurisdictions such as Connecticut and Delaware.

After much legal research, many hearings and large attorney's fees, we were finally able to get court approval to sell the farm. But at what cost! A family that still won't speak to one another and tens of thousands of dollars of legal fees and court costs. All because Mom and Dad's planning was "simple." Too simple.[7]

---

[7] In the trusts that I draft I include a whole section on the powers of the trustees, so that you can decide what they can and can't do. We don't need to go to court.

CHAPTER 14

Will-Based Planning

You will want to base your financial estate planning on a will or a revocable living trust. Which is better for you? Which is too "simple" for your circumstances?

Let's start with wills.

A will contains one's written instructions on how his or her financial affairs are to be handled upon death. It provides directions over what assets are to be distributed to whom and who is in charge. It comes into play only at death and requires a judicial proceeding called a probate. Historically, most people used wills to transfer their property at death, and many people still do.

For a will to operate, it must be probated.

Probate

What is "probate"? Probate is a judicial action filed in state court. The person who will handle the estate, the "personal representative" or "executor," files the original will and a petition with the court, and the court grants the personal representative the authority to administer the affairs of the deceased person under court supervision. I've heard probate sarcastically described as a lawsuit that you file against yourself, with your own money, for the protection of disgruntled heirs and creditors.

The procedure and complications of probate vary widely from state to state. In states such as Montana where the Uniform Probate Code has been adopted, probates are much less burdensome and expensive than in other states. Probate is required if the deceased person, the "decedent," solely owned any real property or more than a certain amount (in Montana $50,000) of personal property, such as vehicles and artwork. Bank accounts, investment accounts, etc., with a beneficiary designation such as POD ("Payable on Death") or TOD ("Transfer on Death") do not require probate. If a decedent owned real property out of state, a separate, "ancillary" probate must also be filed in the state where the property is located.

The Personal Representative pays the decedent's debts, files applicable tax returns, collects any monies owed the decedent, and identifies and values the decedent's assets. If there are no disputes among the heirs, the personal representative then distributes assets after giving the heirs a full accounting and getting the court's approval.

The time required to complete probate proceedings varies depending upon the circumstances, such as the complexity of the estate plan, family issues, and the organization and sufficiency of the decedent's records. Generally, simpler probates range from six months to one year. More complicated probates can take up to two years, or longer.

The biggest expense of a probate is generally professional fees, those of appraisers, accountants and attorneys.

Are there any advantages to probate? Yes, in some circumstances it can be valuable to go through a probate process. For instance, if you have creditors who you think may come after your family when you are gone, by filing a probate you can require them to come forward within a shorter period of time rather than "lying in the weeds" and coming much later to make a claim against your estate.

A Story about a Probate

In my office we don't use wills as often as we did in the past. But we still draft wills for clients with more modest estates whose affairs are not complicated and who do not foresee any family disputes.

Usually this works fine. The personal representative handles the affairs of the estate without objection from anyone and without undue court involvement. The problem is that it's hard to know upfront whether a person's affairs are going to be complicated and whether the heirs really are going to get along.

We prepared a will for a widower with four children. His estate was about one million dollars, comprised of a house, investment accounts, retirement accounts and miscellaneous personal property. The will named his oldest daughter as personal representative and provided that all four kids split the estate equally.

Our client lived till age 92 and passed away at home in his sleep. (That's what I want to do, although I'm shooting for 100 if I can stay reasonably clear-headed and healthy!) We initiated the probate, and everything went fine at first.

The personal representative worked with a local realtor to set an asking price and to decide what we needed to do to make the family home salable. We decided to follow the realtor's advice as to asking price and pre-sale repairs. The personal representative updated her siblings about the sale, and that's when the problems started. Her youngest emailed us, stating that the house was worth more and that it was perfectly salable "as is."

The personal representative was also at work inventorying and dividing up the personal property, which was mostly comprised of furniture, household items, photographs, clothing and some items of (inexpensive) jewelry. Before she got far, her younger sister was emailing her demands about this property. The sister had a full page of personal property items that she wanted, starting with their mother's wedding ring. The personal representative exchanged emails with her sister trying to work things out, but she couldn't get anywhere, and the personal representative got more and more upset. Soon the sisters were not speaking or even emailing one another. Then I got a letter from another attorney advising that his client wasn't satisfied and had instructed him to file a motion with the court to take over control of the estate through "supervised administration." Under this form of probate the court (and all the family members) need to be advised of all the personal representative's planned actions, and the court must approve each one.

To make a long story short, we did eventually get the house sold, the personal property divided and the probate concluded. But the process took over a year and cost the family thousands of dollars of attorney's fees. And the most important result? To this day the sisters are not speaking to one another.

What if my client had used a living trust instead of a will? We still might have ended up in court because under our American system of justice, every citizen has the right to file a lawsuit. But, I'll bet the oldest daughter as trustee could have just followed her father's wishes and administered the trust without interference from her sister.

CHAPTER 15

Living Trust-Based Planning

The alternative to a will is a revocable living trust. A "trust" is an agreement between someone with property (the "trust maker") and someone who agrees to manage the property (the "trustee") for the benefit of someone (the "beneficiary"). There are many types of trusts and many purposes for their creation.

A revocable living trust is a legal arrangement that you set up to hold and eventually distribute your property. While you are able to do so you handle your affairs just as you always have. You are the trustee of the trust, and you are beneficiary. You keep full control and can do anything you could do before setting up the trust. You don't have to seek anyone else's approval or give notice to anyone. I like to say that the trust is invisible till you need it.

The first time you'd need it is if you became incapacitated. With a living trust you can decide ahead of time what should happen and who should be involved. That way you can have as much control as possible and you can avoid a court getting involved in your affairs through a guardianship or conservatorship.

The other time you'd need your living trust is when you pass away. Then the living trust operates like a will—but without having to go through probate.

What are the advantages of a living trust? The fact that a revocable living trust allows you to avoid probate is certainly an advantage. Avoiding probate can mean less legal procedure, less publicity, less chance of a family dispute.

In a probate action, the personal representative must share detailed information with all the heirs and provide an opportunity for them to dispute anything being done before a judge. In some families, this may be especially important because it provides a forum for unhappy family members to question and contest everything done in the estate.

With a living trust, the trustee you have chosen can usually just sit down with professionals such as your accountant and attorney and handle your affairs privately in accordance with your wishes. Trusts are not public documents. At least in Montana they don't have to be registered, including when you pass away. This gives you maximum privacy and avoids court control of your affairs.

There are no breaks in control of your assets in the event of either disability or death. You provide ahead of time what will happen and it happens seamlessly and immediately. This can allow the family business to continue operations without interruptions or court involvement.

A living trust gives you flexibility. You can change your mind at any time. You can amend any part of the trust and end it whenever you wish. You can put property in and take it out, add or remove beneficiaries, change the trustees and sell, give or mortgage the property owned by the trust just as if you owned it outright.

A revocable living trust is also useful if you own real estate in another state. Out of state real estate can pass through your trust so your heirs don't have to file an ancillary probate action in the other state when you pass away. If your planning is based on a will, by contrast, your heirs would have to file a separate ancillary probate action in the every state where you own real estate.

I think the most important advantage is that you can maximize your control if you become incapacitated. In any given year, the chances are much greater that you will become disabled than you will die. Shouldn't your planning reflect that?

With a revocable living trust you decide upfront what should happen if you become incapacitated. First, you determine who should have authority to declare you incapacitated. It won't be some district court judge who has never met you listening to testimony about your mental capacity in open court. Instead, you will likely designate your spouse or another family member to make this decision in consultation with your attending physician. If the person you name can't make this call, then you will have named a backup.

Once the people whom you trust have decided that, at least for now, you're incapacitated, you specify in your trust who is to handle your financial affairs. You're still here but incapacitated, so your trust is still all about taking care of you! Your "incapacity trustee" manages your financial affairs for your benefit when you're unable to do so. Of course you also name backups if that person cannot act.

The result? Without ever going to court—and without any delay—the people whom you trust can handle your affairs.

"Front Loading" Your Planning

A major difference between will-based planning and trust-based planning is how much work you actually do. With a living trust you do more planning and you do more to organize your affairs than if you just do will-based planning. You can call this either a benefit or a disadvantage. I call it a great advantage.

How important is it to you to make everything as easy and as inexpensive as possible for your heirs? For many people that's an important goal. I say that, with living trust-based planning, you are "front loading" your planning. You are making decisions and doing the legwork that otherwise would have to be done by someone else later. This will initially take more time and a bigger investment, but it will give you more control and make things simpler for your heirs. This cannot help but minimize the chance of family disputes and legal wrangling later on.

For example, part of planning with a living trust is reviewing, aligning and documenting your asset ownership. That allows for a much simpler administration of your estate if you become incapacitated or die. (When handling a decedent's estate, we find that one of the most time-consuming and difficult jobs is often just trying to locate assets!)

Are there disadvantages to a revocable living trust? Yes, of course. I would say that the main disadvantage is the extra work and expense upfront because you are "front loading" your estate planning with a living trust. Of course, I see the front loading as an advantage, but I'm not the one paying the legal bill.

You will have to think about your goals and decide if getting this work done upfront is important enough to you to justify the extra time and expense.

Peace of Mind
BY DESIGN

Our Unique Process for Estate Planning

BEGINS HERE

The Right Fit Conversation
FIRST MEETING

The Peace of Mind Protector
ANNUAL REVIEW

The Design Builder
CREATING THE PLAN

The Solution Review
3-MONTH FOLLOW-UP

The Design Solution
DOCUMENT SIGNING MEETING

The Asset Game Plan
FUNDING MEETING

Scott, Tokerud & McCarty, P.C.
Attorneys and Counselors

CHAPTER 16

Our Living Trust Planning Process

Our Unique Process

Here's how our process for trust-based estate planning, **Peace of Mind by Design**, works.

The Right Fit Conversation

We start with The Right Fit Conversation. You and I first have to decide if we are a good fit to work together. This gives me a chance to learn about you and your family, your concerns, and your goals for your planning. It gives you a chance to learn about me and my legal practice. I then describe our planning process, and provide an estimate of what your investment for the planning may be. There is no charge for this step of the process.

The Design Builder

If we decide we are a good fit, we go to work on The Design Builder. We take all the time necessary to unearth and get very clear about your goals and concerns, and we thoroughly explore the issues that may impact your estate planning. Our clients tell us this is the most valuable aspect of our work together. It gives you a chance to get very clear on what you want for your future, your family and your legacy.

Once you've decided what you want to accomplish we discuss the legal "tools" we might use, and together we design a plan to satisfy your concerns and accomplish your goals. I can then quote a guaranteed, all-inclusive price for the entire process. If you decide to go ahead, we enter into an engagement agreement. So, you're not committed until you know exactly what we're going to do and what your investment will be.

The Design Solution

Armed with your "marching orders," my team and I then draft documents for you to review. We prepare diagrams outlining your planning to make sure we're all on the same page: that I've understood your marching orders and you've understood how the planning will work. We then sit down and review the planning documents themselves. Again, we take all the time necessary for you to really understand how the documents work, to make sure the documents address your concerns and goals, and to answer all your questions. When we've done that and made any changes you wish, you can sign the documents.

(Just in case you're a perfectionist like me, my deal with you is that you are free to make reasonable changes within a year at no additional charge. We don't want perfectionism to stand in the way of getting your planning in place.)

The Asset Game Plan

Now we're ready to review your assets and decide what changes in ownership or beneficiary designations should be made to coordinate your assets with your new estate planning. I prepare a detailed spreadsheet listing your assets and your decisions on what is to be done and who is to do it. My team works with your other advisors and the firms where you have accounts to make sure all the "i's" are dotted and the "t's" crossed.

The Solution Review

Generally, at the end of the quarter we schedule The Solution Review. By then you'll have had a chance to think more about your planning and to talk to others. Perhaps there have been some changes in your circumstances. We go over your questions, make any changes to the plan that you wish, make sure your assets are titled appropriately. And make sure you're totally satisfied with your planning.

This is also a good time to share your planning with your family and those you've named to assist. You may be comfortable sharing the details of your planning and your estate with family members, or you may choose only to share certain aspects of your planning, perhaps not disclosing financial information. I strongly believe that there is a lot of value in letting people know about your planning now rather than when you're gone.

I don't have to be involved when you share your planning, but many of our clients have found it beneficial for me to participate in a family meeting. We can meet face to face, on the phone or by "Skyping."

The Peace of Mind Protector

Over time your family circumstances will change. Your finances will change. Your health. And we know that the laws will change, including the tax laws. To make sure your estate plan works the way you want it to, you must periodically review and update it.

Our Peace of Mind Protector is a unique subscription-based program to maintain and improve your planning through yearly reviews and necessary updates.

CHAPTER 17

Taxes

When I first sit down with potential clients and ask about their biggest concerns, almost everyone starts with taxes. I've delayed addressing taxes here because, while they are important, taxes are rarely the most important issue in good estate planning. But I've put it off long enough. Let's talk about the federal and state tax issues that may affect your planning.

The federal taxes are the gift tax, the estate tax, the generation-skipping transfer tax and our old friend, the income tax. The state taxes may include an estate tax or inheritance tax, state gift tax and state income tax.

Federal Gift Tax and Estate Tax

The federal gift tax and the estate tax are "unified." That means that you can't avoid the estate tax just by giving away all your property during your lifetime. There is no limit to how much you can give away, but when you give away more than your gift tax lifetime exemption ($5,000,000 indexed for inflation from 2011; $5,490,000 in 2017), you, the donor, pay a 40% gift tax on any further gifts.

There is an exception to this general rule for smaller gifts. Each year you can give up to the annual gift tax exclusion amount, currently $14,000, to as many recipients as you want free of tax. The gifts won't count against your lifetime exclusion; they'll be out of your estate altogether. This can be a great strategy tax-wise if it otherwise makes sense.

No matter how big the gift is, the receipt of a gift is not income to the recipient, so they don't pay gift tax or income tax on your gift.

You have to report gifts that exceed the annual gift tax exclusion to the IRS. Then, when you die your estate representative must compute how much of your lifetime gift tax exclusion you used up (with gifts of more than $14,000 per recipient in any year) and add that to your estate to compute how much estate tax is owed. It's as if you still owned what you had given away.

(There's good news here, though: what is added back is the value of your gift on the date you made the gift. If you'd kept the property and given it away upon death, the appreciation on the property after the date of the gift would also be in your estate. So, by making the gift you save estate tax on the appreciation.)

The federal estate tax is based on what you own when you die (plus these "taxable" gifts). Your estate representative inventories and values all your property. Your estate will be entitled to deductions, such as for charitable gifts, transfers to your spouse, administration expenses and, most, importantly, the estate tax exclusion amount (currently the same as the gift tax lifetime exemption, $5,450,000). The excess is subject to a 40% tax.

The $5,490,000 lifetime exemptions mean that most families don't have to focus on estate taxes when they do their estate planning and can focus on taking care of themselves and their families the way they want.

Generation-Skipping Transfer Tax

There is another 40% federal tax, the generation-skipping transfer tax, that applies when you leave property to grandchildren or people at least 37.5 years younger than you. It's not an issue for most people though, since, just like with the gift tax and the estate tax, there is an exemption, currently the same as the gift tax and estate tax exclusion amounts. If you make a gift to a grandchild that isn't shielded by the exemption, you pay both the estate tax and the generation-skipping transfer tax on the gift, so a gift could be taxed at 80% when both taxes apply.

Income Tax

Income tax does not apply to lifetime gifts or inheritances. So, your heirs will not pay income tax on what you leave them, no matter how much. (Distributions from IRA's and qualified retirement plans will be income taxed to the recipient later, however, when the distributions are made.)

I discussed how lifetime gifting may be a good strategy to minimize *estate* tax, but now I have to complicate matters by explaining how it can have just the opposite result as to *income* tax. With the high estate tax exclusion amount ($5,490,000 as of 2017) and the top income tax rates at 39% (plus a surtax), the focus in estate planning has changed. The expression among estate planners is: "Income tax is the new estate tax." The majority of Americans don't have to worry about estate tax under current law, so their estate planners need to focus on their exposure to income tax.

As I said above, there is no income tax on a gift or bequest: no problem there. It's when an heir sells an appreciated asset down the road that it makes a big difference whether the heir received the asset at the death of his donor or during the donor's lifetime.

The issue has to do with the income tax "basis" of the asset being sold. Uncle Sam taxes us on the difference between what we sell an asset for and what we are deemed to have paid for the asset, our basis. So, if I bought an asset, then my income tax basis is what I paid for it (with some adjustments like depreciation that we won't worry about here). If I was given the asset, my basis is determined in a different manner. If I received the asset during the lifetime of the donor, then I take his basis. Whatever he paid for the asset, his basis, carries over to me. "Carry-over basis."

By contrast if I inherited the asset, Uncle Sam gives me a break. My basis in the asset is stepped up to the value on my donor's date of death. "Stepped-up basis." Since there is no income tax when I inherit, this doesn't make any difference then. But, when I sell the asset down the road it can make a big difference.

Let me give an example: Say my dad bought 100 shares of XYZ Corporation for $10 a share. If he gave me them to me during his lifetime, my income tax basis is the same as his: $10 per share. So, if I sell the shares for $20 per share, I have capital gains of $10 per share, or $1,000. If my capital gains rate is 15% federal and 6% state, I'll have to pay $210 in capital gains tax.

If my dad held onto the shares till death when they were worth $20 per share and he left them to me, my income tax basis is "stepped up" to the date of death value, $20 per share. If I sell the shares later on for $20 per share, I don't have any capital gain, since my basis is equal to the sales price.

So, by giving me the shares at death rather than during his lifetime, my dad saved me $210 in capital gains tax.

The moral of the story: making a gift of an appreciated asset during your lifetime might not be smart from a tax standpoint.

You have to consider both the effect on the estate and the income tax. It can get a little complicated!

State Taxes

Many states have estate or inheritance taxes. They vary widely. In Montana we're lucky: no state estate or inheritance tax. That doesn't mean the Legislature can't bring it back, but for now Montanans only need to worry about the federal taxes.

CHAPTER 18

Advanced Planning

You may be lucky enough to have an estate of $10 million or more. If so, it's worth thinking about more than basic estate planning.

You may own an investment portfolio with many assets that are challenging to manage even with the help of financial advisors. Over the years you may have developed goals and strategies involving your portfolio that you would like to see perpetuated. How can the family's investments be best managed as you take a less active role? How can the family grow its junior members into good stewards of the family's wealth?

If there is a family business, you have business succession and management issues as we discussed above. Are you ready to start transitioning management responsibility and ownership to family members or employees? How would that all work? If there are multiple businesses, how can they be best operated so that the family's goals are achieved?

All these issues are difficult enough, but the tax issues are especially challenging. Still, for those with larger estates, ample opportunities remain to transfer large amounts tax free to future generations, but time can be a factor. With Congress always looking for more ways to increase revenue, many reliable estate planning strategies may soon be restricted or eliminated. Thus, it is best to put these strategies into place now so that they are more likely to be grandfathered from future law changes when the distributions are made. In our planning tool box we have tools to deal with these issues.

Irrevocable Trusts

The irrevocable trust is one such tool. There are many varieties with exotic sounding names and acronyms like the "ILIT" (irrevocable life insurance trust: pronounced like "eyelet") and the "GRAT" (grantor retained annuity trust).

Let's briefly discuss the ILIT and the GRAT.

Irrevocable Life Insurance Trusts

You have probably heard that life insurance isn't taxable. That's generally true. But only as to income tax, not estate tax. If you have "incidents of ownership" of life insurance, then when you pass away the death benefits will be treated as part of your estate. So, for every dollar of life insurance proceeds that your heirs receive, they must send 40 cents to the IRS.

Wouldn't it be great if your family could receive the full life insurance death benefit and all you had to do was change how you owned the life insurance? That's the idea behind the irrevocable life insurance trust, the "ILIT." We generally suggest an ILIT as the first strategy to consider if, after basic estate planning is in place, we still believe the family will have federal estate tax exposure. ILIT's are relatively straightforward and inexpensive to put into place and manage. They are irrevocable trusts, but we can build in a lot of flexibility to make changes down the road if necessary.

You set up the ILIT as you choose. The insured can't be the trustee, so you'll have to name your spouse, child or someone else whom you trust. You transfer the policies to the trust, but you get the privilege of continuing to pay the premiums! Actually, you'll write the check to the trustee who will turn around and send a trust check to the insurance company to pay the premium.

You specify who the beneficiaries are. Often you'll want the same beneficiaries as you've named in your will or living trust. You also give the ILIT trustee the authority to use the insurance money to assist with estate tax liability. (You do so by giving the trustee the authority to loan money to your estate or to buy assets from your estate.[8]) And, since the life insurance is held in an irrevocable trust, it's not subject to claims of your creditors.

What if you don't have much life insurance? If you have some money to invest it's worth considering life insurance to be held in an ILIT. Whatever you think about the economics of life insurance generally, you should run the numbers. An ILIT investment has an unfair advantage over taxable investments, since there is no income tax and no estate tax to drag down performance.

Grantor Retained Annuity Trusts

Another irrevocable trust in our toolkit is the grantor retained annuity trust or "GRAT." You are setting up the trust so you are the grantor. Let's say you want it to benefit your kids, so they are the beneficiaries. You will pick someone to manage the property, the trustee.

You might transfer a partial interest in the family business, real estate or investments to the trust. The trustee then gives you a promissory note equal to the value of the transferred assets. The note will provide for regular payments back to you, so it is an annuity that

---

[8] For details go to *http://montanaestatelawyer.com/great-falls-mt-estate-planning-ad vanced-estate-planning-lawyer_pa5771.htm.*

you, the grantor, are retaining. Hence, you have a "grantor retained annuity trust."

So, what's the advantage here? Well, first of all, the assets you transferred no longer belong to you. They belong to the trust. So, the assets are protected from any creditors you or the beneficiaries might have.

Designating a responsible trustee allows you to make sure that the assets are responsibly managed and not frittered away.

Plus, since the assets don't belong to you anymore, they won't be subject to estate tax when you die. The annuity you retained will belong to you, but it will normally be worth less than the assets themselves. (The annuity value will often have been discounted based on the structure of the entity and the transaction.)

So, you pick an asset that you think will appreciate, get it appraised, and then transfer it into a GRAT. You receive an income stream for a number of years. Then the trust will distribute the assets to the heirs you have chosen free of estate tax.

Go to our website *www.MontanaEstateLawyer.com*, for more information on advanced planning strategies.

CHAPTER 19

The Cost of Planning

How much does estate planning cost? When an attorney quotes a price, how do you know if it's reasonable? There is no single, right answer, so let me lay out the factors and share my suggestions on how to approach the issue.

First, here are some factors that apply to the cost of any legal work:

- The complexity of the project;
- The amount of time it will take to complete the project;
- The level of expertise required to complete the project with the highest quality;
- The level of risk the attorney assumes by undertaking the project;
- What other attorneys bringing similar expertise, experience and service to the project might charge;
- All legal fees must reflect ethical considerations for billing for professional services. In Montana these are set out in the Montana Rules of Professional Conduct.

The Factors Involved in Estate Planning

When someone asks me what estate planning costs, I compare it to the cost of building a house. What kind of house are we talking about? An 800-square foot A-frame cabin or a 10,000-square foot

McMansion? Do you want hot water heat or electric base boards? Granite counter tops or plastic? Is the builder an experienced, well-regarded contractor or a handyman who wants to branch out into home building?

It's the same for estate planning. What kind of planning are we talking about? Is it just a simple will or is it a comprehensive revocable living trust plan? Do you want to give assets outright to your heirs or do you want to set up protective arrangements to maximize the chance that your property will actually benefit the people you want it to? Will the planning also include making sure that you hold your assets properly and that your retirement account and life insurance beneficiary designations are in sync with the rest of your planning?

The nature of your estate is also a key factor. What do you own and how is it held? Is your estate large enough that the federal estate tax is an issue? How many assets do you own, and how do you hold them? Planning for a farmer with thousands of acres, livestock, equipment and accounts held in different business entities is way more complicated than planning for a retired person with a home, some investments and miscellaneous personal property.

And, finally, who is going to help you? An experienced estate planning attorney or a general practitioner who has a form book for wills and trusts? I tell people right upfront that we are not the cheapest lawyers in town. We think we do a pretty good job, and—if I may say so—we have a lot of satisfied clients, but if getting the cheapest possible price is the most important factor for someone, we're probably not the attorneys for them.

Billing by the Hour or by the Project?

You can pay an attorney to work by the hour or with a fixed price. Which makes most sense for your estate planning?

Hourly billing has its advantages. If the attorney is able to complete his or her work in less time than expected, that means the client will save money. If the attorney is a poor judge of how much time will be required, that won't inflate the cost of the work. But, if the work takes more lawyer time than expected, it is the client who bears the extra expense. The way I think about it, with hourly billing the attorney is shifting the risk of unexpected cost over-runs to the client.

In some cases there are just so many variables and unknowns that the attorney and client can't come up with a fixed price, so they decide on hourly billing. This can happen with certain estate plans with business succession planning included. If you own a business and part of the planning will involve figuring out how and when to transfer the business, there will be a lot of moving parts to your planning! It's hard to know upfront what issues and options you will want to consider in your planning. So, it may be best for you and your attorney to agree that the attorney work on an hourly basis, at least at first.

If you do agree to pay by the hour, you will need to agree to the hourly rate, what expenses the attorney will cover and how frequently the attorney is to bill. Normally the attorney will request a retainer to be applied against the fees to be earned. Hourly rates vary widely. As I write this, rates in my area range from $150 to $400 per hour. The Wall Street Journal reports that New York lawyers charge up to $1,500 per hour!

The other option is using a fixed price. We find that most of our estate planning clients prefer this approach. They want to know what the work is going to cost upfront. I like it because it fits with our model of taking all the time we need to do really good planning. I want to encourage our clients to relax and think deeply about their planning, not worry the whole time we're chatting about "the meter running."

What is the range of fixed fee estate plans? It's all over the place. The problem is to compare apples to apples. I have read of lawyers charging $595 for a revocable living trust. I don't know what they're doing for that price, but I'm sure that they're not spending the time necessary to help the family figure out what's most important to them and which legal tools would work best, and I'm sure they are not "funding" the trust, reviewing and realigning the family's assets to make sure the plan works. For what I consider a full-service engagement I would estimate the range of prices to be from $3,500 to $10,000 or perhaps $12,000 in my area. For very wealthy families with large, complex estates, the price will be more.

If a family with a modest estate wants a plan based on wills, the starting point for a fixed price might be $800 to $1,500, although, again, I've seen ads in newspapers saying a lawyer will charge only a few hundred dollars to prepare a will.

Here's how we address this issue in my office: In the first step of our process, The Right Fit Conversation, we get to know each other, we discuss what your goals and concerns, and I describe how we might address your goals and concerns. Once I have this information and an idea of the makeup of your estate I can usually provide a price range for what the planning might cost.

If we decide we're a good fit and it makes sense to proceed, we move to the second step of our process, The Design Builder. That's when we fully discuss the issues involving you, your family and your estate, and we design a plan together. I then quote a fixed price that covers all the work necessary to put your plan in place, and you can decide if you want to proceed. So, you're not committed till you know exactly what your planning will cost. We think that's the best way to deal with the uncertainty of cost.

Do You See the Value?

So, if there is no one right price for estate planning, how do you know if you're getting good value for your investment?

You can't tell by just looking at your planning documents, although, generally, more detailed documents are better (since you want answers to questions that arise later to come from your planning documents, not some judge). But the technical details of planning documents are complex, and you're going to have to rely on your attorney's expertise to a large extent.

I would suggest that you focus on the process you go through with your attorney and other team members. Does it involve a thorough discussion of the issues that are most important to you and explanations of the different strategies available to you so that you really understand how the planning will work? Does the planning address your biggest concerns and worries in a way that you're comfortable with?

You are investing in your family's future. The important thing is that you feel you're getting good value for your investment. That means that you receive more value than you put in. That's the real measure of what you should pay, and no one can decide what the value is except you.

CHAPTER 20

After You've Signed Your Documents

You're not Done Yet!

Okay, let's say that you and your attorney have designed the estate plan that's right for you, and you've signed the documents. That's where many people (including attorneys) drop the ball, but the job is not done! You and your team still have to make sure your plan will actually work the way you want. That means reviewing how you hold your assets and whom you've named to receive life insurance, bank accounts and retirement accounts. It also means talking to the people you want to be involved in your planning.

Titling Assets Properly

Your plan won't work if you have a trust that has no assets. If your trust says your son gets the cabin, but the cabin actually belongs to your wife, we have a problem. Nor will your estate plan work if your trust says one thing and your life insurance and retirement plan documentation say something different.

So, any good estate planning process must include review of beneficiary designations and how you hold your assets. Of particular concern is any property that is jointly owned. There is more than one way to hold joint property, and it makes a big difference in estate planning. If you own a partial interest in property as a "tenant in common," then whatever you say should happen to the property in your trust will control. If you own a partial interest as a "joint tenant with right of survivorship," it makes no difference what your trust says. If you pass away, your interest automatically goes outright to the other joint tenant.

Your Attorney Should Help

While you can certainly do this work yourself, it's my experience that your attorney and other advisors should help you as part of their estate planning job. Otherwise, once the documents are signed and the binder is put away, it's just too easy for you to move on to something else and not get the job done.

In our office we call this stage of our process "The Asset Game Plan." We hold a separate meeting after the planning documents are signed to discuss how your assets should be held and who will do what to make changes. Our trust funding coordinator then follows up to make sure the work gets done.

You want that kind of process for your planning too.

Share Your Planning

Okay, your estate plan is documented, and the asset ownership and beneficiary designations are just the way you want them to be. Now, to make sure that your plan actually benefits the people you want in the way you want, you need to share your planning.

Sometimes you will have named people to serve as trustees and agents without mentioning it to them. That's fine but when you get the opportunity you should make sure they're willing to serve. You may also have some specific ideas about what to do with your assets that are not in your planning documents. You'll want to share them with your trustees.

Many times you will have named family members as helpers in your planning, whether as successor trustees, agents under a financial power of attorney or healthcare agents. And they will usually be the ultimate beneficiaries of your estate.

This is your estate planning, not your kids'. So, it's up to you plan your estate as you deem best. But, once you've done that, I urge you to let your family know what you've done. That way you can maximize the odds that your plan will work the way you want it to and that there will be no family disputes.

It may just be a matter of explaining your decisions. We see hurt feelings over whom Dad named to handle his affairs, who is to get what, and why Mom or Dad made certain distinctions between family members but never explained why. (Why is Johnny's share's bigger than Sue's? Why should he be the favorite? Why is Bobby named as trustee instead of me? Didn't Dad think I'm responsible?)

All too often Mom signs a living will stating that she doesn't want end-of-life medical care to eat up her estate, but Mom never talks to anyone about this. That can leave the family wondering what she meant, what she really wanted. Did she even read the document before she signed it?

So, there are good reasons for you to share with your family at least some aspects of your planning. You can decide what you want to share but, at a minimum, you should let them know you've done your planning, who is to be in charge if you can't act (and why you've named these people) and what they should do if something happens to you.

Many people are comfortable sharing more, such as how they plan to distribute their estate (and why they've made certain decisions) and even the size and nature of their estate. How much to share is for you to decide but, generally, more disclosure is better than less.

When I think about this issue, I always remember an elderly retired farmer whom I helped with his planning. He was a widower with four daughters. The youngest had been in a number of financial scrapes, and Dad had always bailed her out. So, when he sat down with me to do his estate planning, he directed that her share be reduced to even things up between the daughters. Made sense to me.

Dad died several years later, and I presided over the "reading of the will." All four daughters listened carefully, because their dad had never told them anything about his planning. When I finished, the youngest daughter was visibly upset.

During the probate of their dad's estate, I dealt with all four girls. The youngest daughter's feelings didn't change. She had concluded that her dad didn't love her as much as her sisters. What really surprised—and upset—me was that the youngest wouldn't speak to her sisters. They had nothing to do with their dad's planning, but the youngest daughter took out her upset on her sisters. I did legal work for one of the daughters years later and learned that the sisters had never reconciled.

You don't want that to happen to your family.

It's also useful for your family members to meet with your advisors. They will be working together if something happens to you. You want your family to feel the same sense of confidence in your plan and your advisors that you do.

Learning more about your planning may also spur your family members to do their own planning and to put their own affairs into order.

Your Plan Won't Work if You don't Keep it Updated

The last issue to consider is also one of the most important: you need to keep your planning up to date! No matter how good your plan is, if you don't revisit it from time to time, your plan is not going to work the way you want it to.

Things are going to change. Your family will change. Your health will change. Your finances will change. The laws that relate to your planning—importantly, the tax laws—will change. If your plan doesn't reflect these changes, your family is going to pay the price. You're going to leave money on the table and subject your family to unnecessary complications and expenses.

We think this is so important that we tell prospective clients that we're not the attorneys for them if they won't commit to keeping their plans up to date. We want our clients' plans to work, and we know they won't work if our clients just put them in a drawer somewhere and forget about them.

Conclusion

Start Today

When I hear people cavalierly say that they don't care what happens after they're gone since they won't be here, I get upset. How can they not care what happens to their family? How can they not want to do whatever is possible to make the lives of their kids and grandkids—and communities—better? I just don't get it.

If you've gotten this far in this book I know that you don't share that philosophy. I may not have convinced you that estate planning is one of the most important things you can do and that it can transform you and your family. But I hope I have at least helped you understand how it can give you more control over your own life. And how it can help you make sure your legacy survives, giving your family more control and satisfaction with their own lives.

There's no single right answer about the kind of planning you should do. It's easy to become overwhelmed by all the possibilities. Don't be like my business owner client who kept reading books and attending seminars but would never do any planning because he didn't yet have all the answers. As I finally convinced him: you just need to start somewhere. You don't need to get it perfect the first time. Just keep repeating my mantra: "Estate planning is a process." Any planning you do will be better than no planning. Just pick an attorney and get going!

Once your plan is in place, I guarantee that you will sleep better knowing that you and your family will be okay if something happens to you. You'll have peace of mind.

Glossary of Terms

Advance directive—a document by which a person states his or her wishes as to healthcare decisions so that, if he or she becomes unable to make those decisions, his or her wishes may be known. The documents are typically a healthcare power of attorney and a living will.

Agent—a person authorized to act on behalf of another.

Attorney in Fact—an agent authorized in a power of attorney to perform business-related transactions on behalf of someone else (the principal).

Beneficiary—a person who receives benefits pursuant to a will, trust, or other contract.

Bypass trust—an irrevocable trust commonly created in a will or living trust to pass assets from the first spouse to die to the survivor and then, generally, to the children on the surviving spouse's death. It is structured so there is no estate tax when the trust is established or when it is distributed to the children by using the estate tax exemption.

Conservator—a person appointed by a court to take over and manage the financial affairs of an individual, the "Ward."

Credit shelter trust—another term for a bypass trust (see above).

Decedent—a deceased person.

Estate tax—a tax imposed on the right to transfer property at death.

Estate tax exclusion amount—an exemption from estate taxes that is subtracted from an estate's gross value for purposes of calculating the estate tax. As of 2017 it is equal to $5.49 million.

Executor—a personal representative; the person who administers the estate of a decedent dying with a will.

Fiduciary—a person granted the authority to act for another, the beneficiary. The standard of care requires total trust, good faith and honesty. A personal representative and a trustee are fiduciaries.

Generation-skipping transfer tax—a tax imposed by the federal government on gifts to or for the benefit of family members more than one generation younger than the donor or, if unrelated, on persons who are more than 37.5 years younger than the donor.

Generation-skipping transfer tax exclusion amount—an exemption from the generation-skipping transfer tax that is subtracted from an estate's gross value for purposes of calculating the tax. As of 2017 it is equal to $5.49 million.

Gift tax—a tax on the lifetime transfer of property by one person to another for less than fair market value, while receiving nothing, or less than full value, in return.

Gift tax annual exclusion amount—the amount that may be transferred by gift to one person in a year without incurring a gift tax or affecting the unified credit. It is $14,000 as of 2017.

Gift tax lifetime exclusion amount—the amount that can be transferred by gift from one person over his or her entire lifetime without incurring gift taxes. The amount reduces the amount that can be given away by the individual at death without incurring estate tax. As of 2017 it is equal to $5.49 million.

Guardian—a person appointed by a court to care for the person or property, or both, of an incompetent person.

HIPAA—the Health Insurance Portability and Accountability Act, a law designed to protect the privacy of patients' medical records and other health information.

Incapacity—physical or mental inability of a person to manage his or her affairs.

Inheritance tax—a tax imposed by some states on the assets inherited from a decedent.

Limited Liability Company—a private business entity created under state law that can be taxed as a disregarded entity, a partnership, an S corporation or a C corporation. Its owners are members. It has limited liability for members similar to that of a corporation.

Living Will—an advance directive document outlining a person's desires regarding their medical treatment in extreme circumstances when they are no longer able to state their wishes.

Partnership—an association of two or more co-owners for profit wherein the partners contribute resources, share in profits and losses, and are individually liable.

Personal representative—an executor; the person who administers the estate of a decedent dying with a will.

Power of attorney—a document granting an agent (attorney-in-fact) the authority to act for a person (the principal) in enumerated matters. It is effective only during the lifetime of the principal.

Probate—the state court process to determine if a will is valid and to administer the estate of a decedent in accordance with the will.

Revocable Living Trust—a will substitute that can be altered or canceled by the trustmaker. The trustmaker continues to control and use the property during his or her lifetime, and at the trustmaker's death trust property is transferred to named beneficiaries.

Testator and Testatrix—a man (Testator) or woman (Testatrix) who executes a will.

Trust—an agreement entered into by a person with property (trustmaker, settlor, trustor) with a trustee whereby the trustee agrees to manage property for another person, a beneficiary.

Trustee—an individual or entity granted authority to manage property for a beneficiary in accordance with the terms of a trust agreement. The trustee is a fiduciary.

Will—a document containing a person's (a testator's) wishes concerning transfer of his or her property at death.

Acknowledgments

My thanks go first to Janet Henderson and to Chris Angermann of Bardolf & Company. Their editorial assistance gave me focus, smoothed the rough edges throughout and got me over the finish line. I'd still be floundering without them.

My good friend, Arthur Renander, has supported and encouraged me on the whole project. I couldn't ask for a better friend.

The team at Scott, Tokerud & McCarty freed me up to dedicate the time required for this project. It's great to work with such a cohesive, positive and committed group of professionals.

And, most importantly, the love and continuous support from my wife, Becky, and my daughter, Hannah, keep me going every day. They truly are "the world's greatest wife and kid."

Keith Tokerud, attorney at law, focuses his practice on helping clients protect their families and their wealth and helping his business owner clients plan for the most important financial event of their lives: the transition out of their business.

He is a member of WealthCounsel, a national consortium of estate planning attorneys, the State Bar of Montana's Trust and Estates section and the Cascade County Estate Planning Council.

Born and raised in Great Falls, Montana, Keith earned a bachelor's degree in Russian Studies, magna cum laude, from the University of Pennsylvania. He obtained his law degree from the University of Michigan and initially practiced corporate and securities law in Houston, Texas. When Keith returned to Montana, he worked as a trial lawyer with the Great Falls law firm of Jardine, Stephenson, Blewett & Weaver before joining his father-in-law, Bill Scott, to form Scott & Tokerud in 1986.

Keith has been active in public service. In 2009 he received the State Bar of Montana's Neil Haight Pro Bono Award for his fourteen years of work to obtain political asylum for a political dissident from the Soviet Union.

He has served as chairman of the board of the Great Falls Chamber of Commerce and Big Brothers and Big Sisters of Great Falls. He also served on the boards of the Benefis Healthcare Foundation, United Way of Cascade County, Sister Cities of Great Falls and the Montana/Kazakhstan Exchange Project.

Keith's interests range from playing jazz and classical music to learning foreign languages to backpacking.

For more information go to

www.MontanaEstateLawyer.com